THE SIMON AND SCHUSTER

POCKET GUIDE TO COGNAC & OTHER BRANDIES

NICHOLAS FAITH

A Fireside Book
Published by Simon & Schuster, Inc.
New York London Toronto Sydney Tokyo

THE SIMON AND SCHUSTER POCKET GUIDE
TO COGNAC AND OTHER BRANDIES
Edited and designed by Mitchell Beazley International Ltd,
Artists House, 14–15 Manette Street, London W1V 5LB

A FIRESIDE BOOK
Published by Simon & Schuster, Inc.
Simon & Schuster Building
Rockefeller Center
1230 Avenue of the Americas
New York, NY 10020
FIRESIDE and colophon are registered trademarks of
Simon & Schuster, Inc.

Library of Congress Cataloging-in-Publication Data
Faith, Nicholas, 1933–
The Simon and Schuster pocket guide to cognac and other brandies.

"A Fireside book."
Includes index.
1. Brandy. I. Title. II. Pocket guide to cognac and other brandies.
TP599.F36 1987 641.2'53 87-8443
ISBN 0-671-64231-6

The author and publishers will be grateful for any information which will assist them in keeping future editions up to date. Although all reasonable care has been taken in the preparation of this book neither the publishers nor the author can accept any liability for any consequences arising from the use thereof or from the information contained herein.

Maps and illustrations by Andrew MacDonald
Typeset by Servis Filmsetting, Manchester, England
Printed and bound in Hong Kong by Mandarin Offset

Editor Rachel Grenfell
Coordinating Editor Alison Franks
Designer Tim Foster
Production Androulla Wakefield
Senior Executive Editor Chris Foulkes
Senior Executive Art Editor Roger Walton

CONTENTS

HOW TO USE THIS BOOK

This book is divided into two unequal parts. First is a short section on how brandies are defined, made and drunk; then come a series of sections – first on Cognac and Armagnac, followed by other French brandies and other brandy-making countries. Wherever necessary I have provided a cross-index of the firms and the brands they are making and marketing.

Unless otherwise stated brandies are sold at 40 degrees strength and in containers of 75 centilitres.

The figures given after the names of brands indicate the age at which the owners claim the brandy is sold.

Many expressions recur in the book and most of them are explained in the individual sections. The most important include:

Aguardenta – The Portuguese term for brandy
Aguardiente – The Spanish word for high-proof spirit
Alembic – A word for pot-still (qv) from the Arabic "al-ambic"
Alquitara – The Spanish term for brandy distilled in pot-stills (*see* page 114)
Bagaceira – The Portuguese term for marc (qv)
Bonbonne – A glass jar which holds 25 litres, used for old spirits
Brandewijn, **Brandvin**, **Brandywijn** – A Dutch word for brandy, literally meaning "burnt wine".
Brouillis – Spirit of around 30 degrees produced by the first distillation in a pot-still (*see* page 10)
Chapiteau – Literally a circus-tent, the "big-top". Small round container which traps the alcoholic vapours emanating from a pot-still
Coffey Still – Continuous still (*see* page 10) invented by an Irish exciseman, Edmund Coffey
Col – The neck of a pot-still, often referred to as Col de Cygne (qv)
Col de Cygne – In the supposed shape of a swan's neck
Congeners – The residual chemical components which provide brandy with its flavour, and its drinkers with their hangovers
Destilados – The Spanish word for high-proof spirit (*see also* Aguardiente)
Grappa – Italian version of marc (qv)
Heads – The first spirit to flow from a still. Generally discarded because it is too strong or impure, or both
Holandas – Spirit distilled in Spain, originally to 65–70 degrees for the Dutch market, hence the name
Lees – The detritus, leaves, twigs, skins and other solids left in the vat after fermentation
Limousin – One of the two types of oak used to mature French and other brandies (*see* page 30, *also* Tronçais)
Malolactic Fermentation (le Malo) – Secondary fermentation, during which the malic acid in the wine is transformed into lactic acid
Marc – (*see also* Grappa, Bagaceira, Pomace Brandy) Spirit

distilled either from the lees (qv) left after fermentation or from the pips, skins and stalks left after grapes have been pressed
Oidium – Fungal disease which afflicted many vineyards, particularly in France, during the 1850s
Paradis – Warehouse (chai) used for storing old cognacs
Phylloxera Vastatrix – "Wine louse" which devastated European vineyards during the final quarter of the 19th century
Pomace Brandy – Another term for marc (qv)
Queues – French word for the "tails" (qv) of a distillation
Serpentin – Condenser or cooling-coil used in pot-stills (qv)
Tails – The end of the run of spirit through the still
Tête de Maure – Old form of "Col" (qv) supposedly shaped like a Moor's Head
Têtes – French term for the Heads (qv)
Tronçais – One of the two main types of oak used to mature French brandies (see also Limousin)

INTRODUCTION

We all have our own idea of brandy. The word has so many connotations, above all of a certain sort of fiery warmth, that narrow technical and legal definitions can seem irrelevant. Inevitably any definition sufficiently restrictive to act as the framework for a slim volume such as this one must be partly personal. To me brandy is a distilled spirit recognizably made from the grape. Throughout the book I try to concentrate upon the degree to which the final spirit reflects the nature of the original raw material.

This should not be neutral but bring some positive qualities to the process (although these can be exaggerated. The distillation process concentrates the aromas found in the original grapes, so distilling from varieties like Gewürztraminer or, above all, Muscat, can result in brandies which are too powerfully aromatic to be saleable). The more important the role the raw material plays in the quality of the final product, the more faithful the reflection of its qualities; the less it has been distorted by the distillation process (or by additives) the better the brandy. To me the only other admissible quality is that of the wood in which the brandy has been aged. But even the wood should be a secondary factor. With spirit, as with wine, the grape should take precedence. I sympathized when my old friend Ted Hale refused to buy Rioja for his erstwhile employers: "I buy wine, not oak" he said. The grapiness must never be swamped – as it often is, and not just in Rioja, by the wood.

Without some grapiness, some echo, however distant, of the original fruit, brandy becomes merely a form of vodka, a neutral spirit. This can be useful, as a quick way of seeking oblivion, handy as a mixer, a means of providing warmth or solace against shock, or as medicinal brandy – although even this can be a euphemism. Most of us remember the splendid sight of a prone Groucho Marx demanding in stentorian tones that the assembled company "force brandy down my throat". Obviously my definition excludes all the "brandies" made from other fruits. As we shall see, even the word "recognizably" can have technical implications further limiting the scope of the book.

Burnt Wine

Historically, linguistically, literally the word is simplicity itself. "Brandy" is derived from *brandywijn*, a word of Dutch origin for wine "burnt" in a still to leave the water and remove the alcoholic vapour which condenses back into liquid form, as it cools. In other languages, too, it is the burning which is the essential feature.

Strictly speaking the grapes used to make brandy should have been fermented first into wine. However it seems ridiculous to exclude what are technically known as "pomace brandies" made from the "marc", the pips and skins which remain after the grapes have been pressed, or the lees, the residue left in the vat after the wine has fermented, or even later in the process, (the Germans make a distillate, which they call *hefeschnapps* or *hefebranntwein*, from the lees left after the wine has been racked for the first time). All these spirits evoke echoes of the original raw material far stronger than many so-called brandies, so I have included them.

This is also a recognition that they are the survivors of the peasant tradition of brandy making. At the other extreme is the industrial tradition which detaches the brandy from the place where the grapes were grown. The German brandy makers, for instance, use almost exclusively grapes not grown in their own country. Even the Spaniards use grapes from La Mancha, distilled locally, but matured in Jerez and sold as Jerez Brandy. By contrast, it has been one of the greatest achievements of Cognac to blend the two traditions, the peasant care when making the brandy and the commercial enterprise in marketing it throughout the world.

The Peasant Tradition

At the other extreme from the industrial brandy makers are the hundreds of thousands of thrifty peasants who would never dream of wasting good wine in their stills but who, frugal as they have been forced to be throughout the ages, salvage their marc and lees and make marc with it. Happily, some consumers can still tell the difference. In Italy there are a handful of honest, competent firms each making large quantities of brandy distilled from all manner of grapes, which the Italians consume in large quantities. But they do not lavish any emotions on their brandies. Their love is reserved for the grappas, the marc made by a scattering of smaller distillers from local grapes.

The EEC now recognizes the legitimacy of the *artisanal* marc, and includes it in the definitions proposed in October 1986 outlined below. These impose a number of important quantitative limitations upon brandy makers. The first is the strength of the spirit when first distilled, reflected in the quantity of flavoursome solid substances (technically known as congeners) retained in the alcohol. The stronger the original distillate, the more it has been cleansed, purified, rectified, the lower the proportion of aromatic sediment and the less the final product resembles its raw material. The EEC's rule is a useful one. Despite this the quantities must not be exaggerated. By the EEC's definition, a 70 centilitre bottle of brandy must contain not less than 0.56 grammes (less than one-fiftieth of an ounce) of solid matter.

Industrial Stills

The industrial continuous stills (described on pages 00 and 00) normally produce a spirit of up to 96.6% alcohol. I have excluded brandies composed principally of spirit distilled to this concentration, because they resemble other flavoured neutral spirits, such as blackcurrant vodka, rather than brandies made from grapes. The EEC has proposed a cut-off point of 86%. This is the limit for some countries (eg. Italy and Germany); well below the 95% to which some cheap Spanish brandies are distilled. Nevertheless I have included them, having "nosed" the resulting raw spirit. Even a variation of about one degree, between 95% and 96.6% pure spirit, provides a perceptible difference. The 95% spirit retains a hint of its origins.

These definitions are not easy to maintain, if only because information is so difficult to come by. Brandy is mysterious stuff, even to most of those employed by the companies who sell it. Many companies did not bother to return the questionnaires we sent them, so, totally inadvertently, we have excluded many brandy producers we look forward to welcoming in the second edition of the guide. The replies that did arrive varied in helpfulness. It does not help greatly to learn that Messrs Ernest and Julio Gallo make the best-selling brandy in the United States, but that was all the information the Gallos were prepared to divulge. No one else was quite so uninformative. It may be that we have excluded brandies which the makers affirm are made to the EEC's new standards. Should this be so, upon confirmation, their names will be included in a future edition.

THE EEC'S PROPOSED DEFINITIONS (10 OCTOBER 1986)

"Wine Spirits"
– a spirit designed for human consumption produced by the distillation at less than 86% volume solely of wine or wine fortified for distillation or by the redistillation of a distillate of wine at less than 86%, with no added ethyl alcohol,
– containing more than 125 grams per hectolitre of pure alcohol of volatile substances other than ethyl and methyl alcohol, and a maximum of 200 grams of methyl alcohol per hectolitre of pure alcohol.

"Brandy" or "Weinbrand":
follows the definition of "Wine Spirit" but must contain more than 200 grams per hectolitre of pure alcohol, of volatile substances, other than ethyl and methyl alcohol and must be aged for at least one year in oak receptacles or for at least six months in oak casks holding less than 1,000 litres.

"Grape Marc" or "Marc Spirit":
– produced exclusively by the distillation of grape marc, with or without added water, to which may be added a percentage of lees (their exact proportion yet to be fixed).
– distilled at less than 86% volume, so that the distillate retains the aromatic principles of the raw materials used.
– contains a total quantity of volatile substances other than ethyl and methyl alcohol exceeding 140 grams per hectolitre of pure alcohol and a maximum of 1,000 grams of methyl alcohol per hectolitre of pure alcohol.

"Grappa":
– follows the definition of "marc", but must have at least 240 grams of volatile substances per hectolitre of pure alcohol and must be aged for at least one year (though the rule does not specify that the container must be of wood).

HOW TO MAKE BRANDY

In theory distillation is the simplest of physical processes. It is based on the fact that alcohol and water boil at different temperatures, water at 100°C, alcohol at 78.3°C. If a fermented liquid is heated, the vapour containing the alcoholic constituents is released first. It can then be trapped and cooled, then condensed to an alcoholic liquid.

The phenomenon was probably first observed by the Arabs, who carried the torch of science during the Dark Ages. We still use their words: al-ambiq (alembic) for the still, al-kuhl (alcohol) for the distillate. Originally, the object was to produce medicinal essences, but it was soon discovered that the use of an appropriate raw material produced a drinkable liquid, a "water of life", *aqua vitae*. But the raw materials were generally so impure that the alcohol could only be consumed with safety if it had been repeatedly redistilled, which removed most of the essential characteristics of the original raw material as well.

Qualitatively, the biggest breakthrough came in the 16th and early 17th centuries when it was found that distilling the sharp white wines, produced on the slopes overlooking the little town of Cognac in western France, resulted in spirits which, after as few as two passes through the stills, produced and eminently drinkable brandy, especially if aged for a few years in oak casks. It has proved to be an unbeatable formula.

The Grapes

The first key to Cognac's success is the nature of the wine: the grapes used in the best brandies must have some character and be relatively weak and acid. The ideal balance was found in the Folle Blanche, an acid, aromatic grape used both in Armagnac and Cognac in the 19th century. Unfortunately, it proved unsuitable for grafting on to the American rootstocks used after phylloxera had attacked the vineyards – the bunches of grapes were all too susceptible to grey rot and too tightly packed to be reachable even by modern antirot sprays. So in Cognac, and now increasingly in Armagnac, the Folle Blanche was replaced by the higher yielding, more amenable (and markedly less characterful) Ugni Blanc.

Unfortunately, only a few distillers have the means and patience to try alternative varieties, or to accept that a little Folle Blanche is better (even if more expensive) than a lot of Ugni Blanc. The balance is a delicate one: the Colombard, much favoured in Cognac in the 18th century, is a little too fragrant to be an ideal base wine. Yet there are alternatives: in Catalonia Mascaro and Torres (*see* page 123) are showing what can be done with the well-balanced local variety, Parellada. Cognac's dominance could be challenged – though since it takes up to 40 years for the full qualities of a brandy to emerge, any challenger must possess immense reserves of capital and patience.

Slow and Gentle

The next essential factor in making fine brandy is the speed of distillation: the slower, the gentler, the more effectively the aromatic elements in the raw material are detached with the alcohol, the better. It is rather like stewing fruit: the lower the flame on the stove, the more intense the aromas released and the more thoroughly is the residue drained of them. Indeed, the Cognaçais like to describe their method of distillation as (speeded-up) evaporation.

They are right: the vapours should contain as high a proportion as possible of the congeners, the hundreds of organic chemical compounds which are extracted with the alcohol. Some of these are undesirable, bringing with them rank and unpleasant aromas, and have to be removed. This entails a close control over the distillation process to remove the "heads", the first vapours emerging from the still, which contain the bulk of these undesirable elements, and then the "tails" which will simply be too feeble, without the requisite alcoholic concentration.

Any method of distilling or cooking the wine must be both gentle and controllable. These requirements conflict with economic reality since the ideal involves the slow, gentle distillation of small batches of wine. The wine used to make cognac is heated twice in pot-stills holding not more than 30 hectolitres of wine; once to turn the wine (which has an alcoholic strength of 8 to 9%) into a *brouillis* of about 30%, and then into brandy up to 72%.

At the other extreme are the continuous stills, invented early in the 19th century by, and named after, an Irish exciseman called Coffey. This still (illustrated on page 11) can concentrate wine 10 or more times up to the normal industrial maximum of 96.6%. This fast, continuous process saves heat (pot-stills have to be reheated between each batch), is highly productive – and can be highly destructive of all the elements which make brandy interesting.

The Cognac still (described on pages 26–29) remains the ideal method of extracting the essentials from wine. The Coffey still is much more brutal in its treatment of the wine: the process is far quicker – a matter of minutes where each stage in the production of cognac can last up to eight hours. In the Coffey still, moreover, the hot wine is mixed with steam to help extract the alcohol, thus further coarsening the process. It can be controlled only roughly, with a fixed percentage of the heads being removed. Nevertheless there is no need for the alcohol to emerge at 96.6%. The strength of the final distillate can be adjusted simply: the greater the

The continuous still

The continuous still has two columns. Cold wines enter at **1** and passes down the coil in the rectifier, the right-hand column, being heated by hot vapour rising from **8**. The hot wine leaves the rectifier at the bottom and rises up to the top of the second column, the analyser, at **2**. Then it falls onto perforated plates in the analyser. Hot steam enters at **5** and rises, causing volatile parts of the hot wine to boil away. They escape as vapour via **6**. The water in the hot wine boils at a higher temperature so it falls down the analyser to escape via **7**. The spirit vapour from **6** enters the bottom of the rectifier at **8**. It rises, and is cooled by the incoming wine. Less volatile elements (feints) condense and escape as liquid via **12**, to be pumped back to the top of the analyser at **13** to go through the process again. The spirit alone reaches the top of the rectifier as vapour. It is cooled by a cold radiator at **9** and flows out of the still at **10**. Very volatile elements emerge as vapor at **11**.

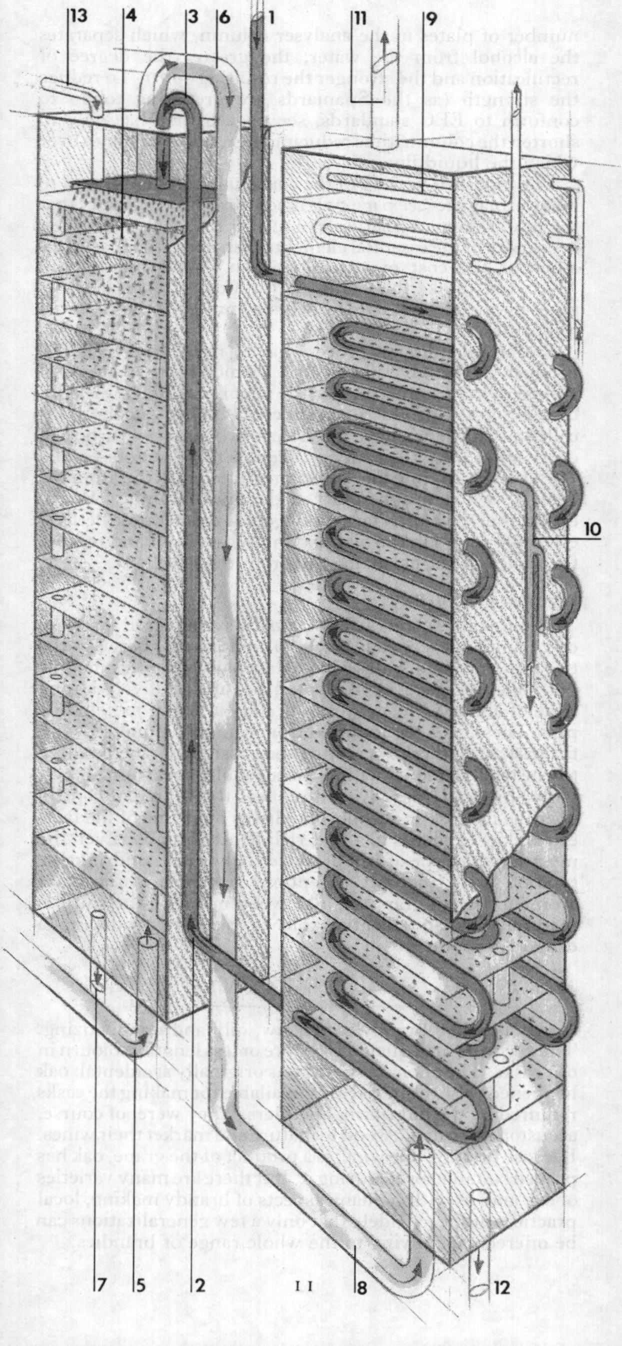
13
4
3
6
1
11
9
10
7
5
2
8
12

number of plates in the analyser column, which separates the alcohol from the water, the greater the degree of rectification and the stronger the resulting spirit. To reduce the strength (as the Spaniards are preparing to do to conform to EEC standards, see page 8) one has only to shorten the column, thus reducing the number of plates over which the liquid flows.

The modified version of the continuous still employed to make armagnac (*see* page 70), is so primitive, so rustic, that the raw armagnac emerges at a mere 52%, thus preserving even more of the essential elements than does a Cognac still – albeit at the cost of requiring even longer maturation. Moreover, unlike the Coffey still, it does not use steam to separate the alcohol, which helps to preserve the essential impurities.

But any distillation process has to result in a balanced product. Although ethyl alcohol – which has two atoms of carbon in every molecule – is the major product of the still, distillation also produces a number of "higher" alcohols, so-called because they have more than two atoms of carbon in every molecule. Their higher alcohols turn into oils, called "fusel oils". In time these are transmitted into the aromatic "esters" which are the glory of the finest brandies. But in excess they give off a tarry, pungent aroma. Other "ethyl" esters are found in the distillation process itself and require the same sort of balancing out from the distiller.

Alternative Stills

There are other choices. The *calandre* system used for Marc de Champagne (*see* page 105) is a compromise between the two systems already described. In Spain examples include pot-stills (*see* page 113) adapted to turn relatively strong wine of about 12 to 14% into brandy at 65 to 70% in one pass. These use a rectifying coil, or chamber, connected with the basic still, thereby creating the possibility of redistilling the heavier elements within the alcoholic spectrum. Inevitably any single-pass system reduces the degree of control over the process as a whole and distils out some of the fatty esters, key elements in a full, rich, fruity brandy. Even the most suitable type of still produces only a raw, undrinkable type of spirit (the only exceptions are some of the more aromatic Italian grappas). The wood in which the spirit is matured has an essential role to play in producing a drinkable product.

HOW TO MAKE MATURE BRANDY

Newly distilled brandy tastes raw, oily and unappetizing. The key to its final quality is a more or less lengthy sojourn in oak casks. The choice of wood was originally accidental: oak happened to be the most easily available for making the casks required by the pioneering distillers. They were, of course, accustomed to using wood to mature and market their wines. Because brandy, like wine, is a product of the grape, oak has proved suitable for maturing it. But there are many varieties of oak and, as with so many aspects of brandy making, local practices differ so widely that only a few generalizations can be offered as applying to the whole range of brandies.

Most of the qualities which make oak so suitable are physical. For whatever the chemical qualities of the wood and the reactions they induce when in prolonged contact with the spirit, it is the porosity of the cask which allows the brandy to have a steady, limited access to the air. The brandy gradually absorbs the oxygen required to oxidize and thus soften the raw spirit.

Some oaks are more porous than others: but, physically, the type (and age) of the wood are less important than the size of the cask. The smaller the cask the greater the exposure of the brandy to the wood – and the air. More exposed are the Spanish brandies, matured in the solera system, which are often poured from cask to cask.

By no accident the best brandies are matured in casks holding 400 litres or less. No serious brandy maker pretending to offer a spirit of any individual quality should be using the vast vats containing 100 hectolitres seen in many distilleries. Such brandy makers inevitably rely upon additives to compensate for the blandness and lack of individual qualities in the spirit itself; they probably use *boisé* – oak chips soaked in old spirit and immersed in the new brandy for a few months – to simulate a genuine ageing process. Inevitably *boisé* brandies are harsher than those whose contact with the wood has not been artificially accelerated.

The Effect of Oak

Nevertheless the chemical constituents of the oak have a part to play in the maturation process. This varies considerably with different brandies. Those matured in large casks made of old wood, from which the tannins and lignins have long been extracted, are not as enriched as say, those (including most cognacs) which have had a spell in small, new oak casks immediately after distillation.

There are so many chemical elements in the brandy – up to three hundred have been detected – that any of them can react with the tannins and the lignins in the oak. The soluble lignins bring with them the lovely lingering aroma of vanilla which distinguishes the finest brandies. The tannins provide the brandy with its colour and its woodiness, which can be overwhelming if the original spirit was not fruity enough.

The same principles apply when considering the maturation of wine in cask, except that brandies remain in wood for up to 40 years, 10 times as long as the most traditional Rioja or Barolo. As always, tradition is costly: it assumes that the brandy maker has all the time in the world, does not have to worry about cash flow, or the return on capital invested in brandy and the – increasingly expensive – casks. Fortunately there are enough conscientious firms (and enough discerning drinkers) to make the effort worthwhile.

HOW TO ENJOY BRANDY: GULP, MIX – OR SIP

The classic picture of the brandy drinker is a gentleman, usually elderly, lowering a substantial nose into an enormous balloon glass containing a sticky-looking, dark brown liquid, presumably cognac. Good publicity for the status of brandy, but most misleading.

Firstly, most brandies (even more so marc) are gulped by drinkers looking for warmth. The warmer the better, a touch of sweetness does not matter, the drinker is looking merely for consolation in the form of a mixture of velvet and fire. The Spanish brandy makers, in particular, perfectly understand the requirements of a docker looking for a quick shot on a dank, icy January morning on his way to the quayside at Bilbao. This is why Fundador, itself a synonym for Spanish brandy in Anglo-Saxon countries, is so popular.

Another substantial proportion of brandies is mixed into cocktails and long drinks.

Only a minority of brandies is interesting enough to be cherished, to be sniffed and sipped, rather than gulped or mixed. The general run of brandies are like most wines, adjuncts to life, not an important phenomenon in their own right. But the fine armagnacs, the best Spanish brandies, as well as the finest cognacs, and a few others from Portugal and the United States are worth care and consideration.

The Nose

The key is the nose: for even the most heroic imbiber can only drink a limited quantity of brandy. The most abstemious can sniff endlessly, thus absorbing the fruity subtleties of the brandy, guessing the age, the type of wood, enjoying the whole phenomenon before taking even the first sip.

For the greatest enjoyment one needs an appropriate glass, convivial company and time. Brandy is thought of as a masculine drink, but women, with their more sensitive noses, are generally better tasters than men, because so much more depends upon the aroma than on the taste.

Glasses

Proper tasting depends on finding a suitable shape of glass. The principle is very simple: the glass must be of a shape which allows the aromas to be concentrated before they hit the nose, and big enough to allow them to develop. It must not be too big, or it will require a lot of brandy to provide the aromas to fill the air in the glass. Unless you are proposing to offer your guests quite disgustingly large amounts, enormous balloons are decidedly out. At the other extreme avoid the tiny thimbles which leave no room for the brandy to develop its aromas. These limitations are arbitrary. In Cognac the professionals use tulip-shaped glasses. I sometimes use a wineglass, or, if only a tiny quantity is to be tasted, a champagne flute. Small balloon glasses, which can be twiddled as you contemplate and talk, are fine. The best of all is the glass called the *Impitoyable*, designed and produced by a M. Jacques Pascot in Burgundy. As the name implies, the glass is designed to reflect faithfully all the elements in the liquid. The result can be a pitiless exposure of some defect which would not have been detected in a less rigorous container. That is half the fun of tasting brandy.

Mix and Enjoy

The picture of the traditional brandy drinker has deterred too many people from using brandy as a mixer, although it mixes well, far better than whisky. If one is taking a mixed drink before a meal at which wine is to be served, it makes more sense to use brandy rather than whisky as a base, to avoid mixing grape and grain.

It is idiotic to waste a good brandy, but anything up to the VSOP level serves splendidly. The only question is that of sweetness. If one is mixing the brandy with something sour, like lemon juice, one can use less sugar by employing a richer, Spanish-type brandy. If the recipe calls for cream, then clearly a dry brandy, like a cheap young cognac, is in order. Personally I cannot stand the type of creamy brandy drink immortalized by the Brandy Alexanders so lovingly consumed by Anthony Blanche in *Brideshead Revisited*. I find any brandy rich, and prefer cutting it with something sharp.

In his invaluable *Larousse des Cocktails*, Jacques Sallé very sensibly divides his recipes into types based upon a handful of basic mixtures. Two are simple long drinks: the old country-house favourite, B and S, brandy and soda, suitable also for Perrier, which adds an agreeable touch of saltiness and makes a far more refreshing drink than neat mineral water; and the other old standby, ideal for cold winter afternoons, the Horse's Neck, brandy and ginger ale, with a drop of Angostura Bitters and a twist of lemon peel (If one is using the much sweeter American ginger ale a drier brandy is required).

I feel faintly sick even describing Brandy Alexander, made with chocolate and cream, and its variants (Alexander's Sister, or Alexandra, which use coffee instead of chocolate); even more nauseating (to me, but why agree with me?) are the many cocktails made from a base of brandy and banana cream, to which can be added *crème fraiche* or even Royal Mint Chocolate (as in Ross Royal, invented in 1969 by a Mr Bryan Ruddy).

Brandy and Lemon

Much more palatable are the wide range of drinks taking advantage of the affinity which brandy has for fresh lemon (splendid for cutting the richness of sweeter brandies) or drinks made from, or tasting of, oranges, like Cointreau or Grand Marnier. The two are combined in the classic Side Car, two portions of brandy to one each of Cointreau/Grand Marnier and fresh lemon juice. Eliminating the orange flavoured drink and adding sugar leaves one with the delicious Brandy Sour. Brandy goes equally well with fresh orange juice, with or without Cointreau/Grand Marnier or, a splendid combination, with lemon juice and Mandarine Napoléon, itself rather sticky, but a splendid mixer.

There are brandy-based drinks for every time of the day. Even at breakfast one does not have to confine oneself to a quick slug of neat brandy. Sallé has a recipe for Breakfast Nog, which combines brandy, Grand Marnier/Cointreau, milk and an egg. Have a nice day!

COGNAC

Man and Nature in Harmony

For the past three centuries cognac has been almost universally recognized as the finest of all the hundreds of spirits distilled from grapes. For sheer depth and intensity, fruitiness, subtlety of the bouquet, warmth and complexity of flavour and length of time for which the taste lingers on the palate, cognac remains incomparable. The ability to extract so much of the essential flavours from the grape is no accident. It involves possessing the right soil and climate, choosing the right grape varieties, using the appropriate distillation methods, and then enhancing the inherent quality through long storage in the right kind (and size) of wooden cask under the right (damp, dark) conditions.

Yet even this complicated formula would not have sufficed if the Cognaçais – ironically a notoriously closed-in, culturally introverted breed, their qualities epitomized by their nickname *Cagouillards*, snails – had not been prepared to exploit their historic access to markets likely to appreciate the fine – and therefore by definition expensive – spirit they produced. The Cognaçais needed to be both lucky and clever.

The Historical Background

In the last 40 years of the 17th century the fashion-conscious world of Restoration London, like so many others before and since, lived largely in public. The "Café" society congregating in the capital's innumerable coffee houses experimented with a whole host of new drinks. Some, like tea, coffee and chocolate, were non-alcoholic. Most were wines: claret, port, sherry, more or less fortified to withstand the journey to Britain (and to accord with the English taste for robust liquors). Only one, from Cognac, a small town in western France, was a spirit. Since that day Cognac has never looked back.

From newspaper advertisements at the turn of the 18th century we can measure precisely – simply by the prices at which they were offered – that the brandies from "Coniac" were worth at least one-tenth more than those from Nantes, La Rochelle or Bordeaux. In the chapter on the making of cognac I explore the unique qualities which have ensured cognac's dominance, the geographical and geological background, and analyse the methods used, then as now, to make cognac. But history has also taken a hand to help the town.

Even today it is relatively small, with little more than 20,000 inhabitants. In the 17th and 18th centuries, before the town burst its medieval walls, it held only 5,000. The old town on the bank of the River Charente remains a charming medieval jumble, its sturdy, handsome houses only gradually being cleaned and modernized by the Cognaçais (after a handful of Englishmen working for Cognac firms have led the way).

Originally the town was important as a crossing over the river, but in the Middle Ages became a notable trading centre for salt, the region's first staple export, and then for wine. They provided Cognac with an incomparable network of contacts in northern Europe, since both depended on markets in Britain, the Low Countries and Scandinavia. Although Britain became far and away the most important market for wine in the 12th and 13th centuries, contact was not lost with other markets. The trade was well organized. Local brokers throughout the Saintonge – the region from Angoulême to the sea – would buy the salt or wine on behalf of foreign buyers. The casks were shipped down the Charente to Tonnay-Charente, the tidal limit down-stream, on board *gabares*, the special barges used for 700 years, until well into the 20th century. In the port of La Rochelle they were sold to the representatives of the foreign buyer. This pattern remained the same when cognac replaced the wine and salt trade. It was not until the late 19th century that the merchants grew rich enough to hold more than one or two years' stock of cognac. Until then they remained, effectively, brokers. The growers matured the cognacs, shipped them in cask, the eventual buyers financing the purchase, which they bottled under their own names.

In the long term the Cognaçais were equally lucky in being liberated by the French from British control in the 14th century, nearly a hundred years before their great rivals in Bordeaux. In the short term the Cognaçais lost their most important market. They were forced to diversify their outlets and thus, in the very long term, their products as well. Two hundred years later they were well placed to satisfy a new demand, for *brandywijn*, a wine which had been burnt, the old word for distillation. This trade arose in the last half of the 16th century when the Dutch, fast becoming the dominant commercial force in Western Europe, needed concentrated wines for their sailors to render palatable the generally putrid drinking water in their ships. At first they imported the wine from the Saintonge to "burn" in Holland in copper stills imported from Sweden. The Dutch authorities disliked using precious grain, the alternative raw material for spirits, because it was an important staple food. As the demand grew, the Dutch started "burning" the wine nearer its source.

Until the mid-17th century the wine used generally came from the *Bois*, slopes which, as the name implies, had been wooded originally. The *Bois* had turned to grapes because they were not as suitable for growing grain as the Champagnes, the semicircle of rolling uplands south of Cognac. The locals quickly imitated the Dutch, although for over a century they valued the Dutch stills more highly than their own. By then what had been a practical necessity for the Dutch became a much-valued luxury in fashionable London. From then on cognac's reputation was safe, provided only that it retained its original production methods and the qualities which had made it famous. These criteria, much the same today as they were then, are analysed on pages 25–33. It was the combination of Charentais conservatism and solidity which ensured continuity.

The tradition of quality developed slowly but steadily, in keeping with the local temperament. During the 17th century the Champagnes were covered in vines – and it was found that they produced better grapes than the *Bois*, just as they had produced better grain. By the time of the French

Revolution the last area devoted to growing grapes for wine – the Borderies, an oblong of land just north of Cognac – had succumbed. Their sweet wines had been much prized but a terrible frost in 1766 enabled their rivals in Sauternes, south of Bordeaux, to replace their offerings.

Even before the French Revolution the Cognaçais and their trade were not unduly hampered by feudal restrictions. In the early 13th century the unlucky King John, ruler of western France as well as of England, had granted the town its freedom (one reason why Cognac, rather than Jarnac, eight miles further upstream, gave its name to the drink). Three centuries later Cognac's freedom had been reinforced by its most distinguished native, King Francis I, the very model of a Renaissance monarch, born in Cognac in 1493.

After his death the Cognaçais were badly affected by religious wars because Jarnac, in particular, was a centre of Protestantism, and the scene of a crucial battle. But the reputation as a Protestant redoubt provided a natural link with the Huguenot mafia, which was so important in Western European trade. Even in the 18th century, when Protestants were, officially, not tolerated, the Cognaçais refused to help the local authorities to search them out. The whole region was, by 18th century French standards, socially homogenous and relatively prosperous. Famous firms, such as Martell, Delamain and Hennessy, are still run by the families which founded them in the 18th century.

So in 1789 the locals were preoccupied, not by news from Paris of the end of the Ancien Régime but with the frost of the previous winter, which would have reduced the townspeople to starvation had it not been for the charitable intervention of some of the wealthier local merchants, notably M. Martell. As relative outsiders to the French feudal system the Cognaçais were largely unaffected by the Revolution, and during the Napoleonic period they were hurt only by the periodic attempts to interfere with trade with Britain, their best market. It was during the Napoleonic era that Martell and Hennessy first gained the supremacy which they have never subsequently lost.

Nineteenth Century Prosperity

Nevertheless the defeat of Napoleon in 1815 was a great relief – ironically so in view of the use the Cognaçais were to make of his name a century later. In the following decades the town burst beyond its medieval walls for the first time, and newly rich merchants like Messrs Otard and Dupuy built large houses in the woods of the new town. Even so Martell and Hennessy retained their pre-eminence. It was they, most crucially, who set the price at which the growers would sell their brandies to the merchants. For the basic pattern persisted: growers and merchants formed hereditary relationships, they were bound, not by contracts, but by the habit of regularly trading, over generations, an agreed style of cognac. In 1857 the merchants' position was strengthened by a new law which allowed them to register their trademarks and thus assert their own individuality. Previously, most cognacs, especially in Britain, had been sold under the names of the merchants who imported them in cask, rather as buyers' own brands are today.

But it was free trade, or rather the reduction of customs duties by the British in 1861–62, which heralded a brief period of glory when sales tripled in 15 years to 450,000 hectolitres – nearly 65 million bottles – annually. Britain was the biggest market, but everywhere in the world, from Latin America to Tsarist Russia, cognac became the most fashionable of spirits. This prosperity was doomed, for production rose even faster than consumption. The Charente became, briefly, the biggest vineyard in France, and thousands of acres of marginal land were planted with vines. The threatened crisis of overproduction was averted, however, by an even worse disaster: the onset of that infamous louse *Phylloxera vastatrix*, which arrived in the Charente in 1871 and spread to the whole vineyard by the end of the decade.

The plague ended the hundred years of independence enjoyed by growers, especially in the Champagnes. Their stocks grew ever more valuable as the devastation spread, but they could not survive the 20 years or more it took for the vineyards to be replanted. The delay was partly viticultural: a decade or more was required to ferret out American root stocks suitable for the chalky soil of the Charente. It was only in the late 1880s that the proper source was found – in Texas, where a local nurseryman, T.V. Munson, had cultivated the wild vines of the Red River. The delay was also psychological: the growers in the Charentes, as elsewhere in France, hoped they could retain their precious French vines by treating them with chemicals; moreover, they simply could not afford to buy the new plants.

So the better-financed merchants got the upper hand. They were not exploitative: they could have bought up all the best vineyards at prices one-tenth of those prevailing in the golden days of the 1860s. In fact, they led the way in replanting grafted stocks and helped the growers with advice, plants and fertilizer. They had their own struggles, mainly against the frauds which had besmirched the good name of Cognac in the years of shortage. They (and the champagne merchants of Reims and Epernay) were in the forefront of the battle to protect their good name, both inside and outside France. For the Cognaçais, the battle against imitators was largely settled by legislation in 1905, reinforced in 1929 by the special *Acquit Jaune d'Or*, the gold-coloured certificate of origin which accompanies every load of cognac on the public highway.

Replanting and protection from imitators, however, did not restore prosperity. After World War I came Prohibition in the United States, regulatory state monopolies in Canada and Scandinavia, and crippling (albeit temporary) duties in Britain. The outlook was so bad that in 1922 Martell and Hennessy made a 25 year pact to work together, taking shares in each other's firms, effectively carving up the world's major markets between them.

Ironically it was the German Occupation of 1940–1945 which provided the springboard for postwar cooperation and prosperity. Naturally the town was occupied, but controlled by a sympathetic figure, one Herr Klaebisch, who had been at school in Cognac before World War I. His family had controlled the well-known firm of Meukow, one of the many engaged in the lucrative trade through the

Hanseatic ports with Scandinavia and Eastern Europe. Klaebisch tried to minimize the disturbance to the Cognaçais, although they had to provide the Germans with enormous quantities of brandy (the Cognaçais cheated, of course, by shipping a lot of spirit made from root vegetables, thus preserving their stocks of real cognac).

During the war Maurice Hennessy and a well-known grower, Pierre Verneuil, followed the example of the growers and merchants in Champagne by working together to form what emerged after the war as Cognac's governing body, the Bureau National Interprofessionel du Cognac. The BNIC, composed equally of growers and merchants, acquired a great deal of de facto independence from the government in the formulation and supervision of the rules governing Cognac, which had already been laid down before the war (*see* Definition of Cognac, page 34). Within Cognac the BNIC took over the role, previously performed by Martell and Hennessy, of deciding the price for new brandies from the various *crus*. The region had been divided into *crus* in the 1930s as a natural consequence of the system of *Appellation d'Origine Contrôlée* envisaged in the original statute protecting regional names and which became law in 1905. These definitions, which provoked what amounted to civil war in Champagne, were carried through without any argument in Cognac, largely because the basic divisions had been foreshadowed by the market since the 18th century. They were first defined on the map in the 1860s by a pioneering geologist, M. Coquand.

The end of World War II ushered in nearly 30 years of increasing prosperity. The BNIC greatly improved the relationship between growers and merchants, and was in turn lubricated by that prosperity. The biggest changes were in the structure of the major firms. In 1947 Martell and Hennessy did not renew their partnership agreement. Martell remained independent, but in 1971 Hennessy merged with the Champagne firm of Moët & Chandon. The Big Two became the Big Four through the growth of Courvoisier and Rémy Martin. Courvoisier was established in the late 18th century and made its name by using the Napoleonic symbol in the years before World War I. In the postwar boom its sales outran its stocks and in 1964 it was taken over by Hiram Walker, the Canadian liquor firm, the first outsider to gain a substantial foothold in Cognac. As the analyses of individual houses show, other intruders swiftly followed, the most important being the Distillers Company who took over Hine in 1971. Rémy Martin (*see* page xx) grew rapidly without the benefit of outside capital. It was the creation of two powerful local figures, André Renaud, son-in-law of a major grower, and his own son-in-law André Hériard-Dubreuil. They introduced a new idea of focussing their appeal solely upon cognacs made in the Champagnes.

It was natural for Hériard-Dubreuil, a master tactition, to support the growers from the two Champagnes in the farcical "Cognac War" of 1970, which the locals took more seriously than did the outside world. The "war" was sparked off by the decision of the other major companies to omit the word "Champagne" even from their better cognacs. Their reasoning was obvious: they were master blenders, who relied greatly on cognacs from the Borderies (which were no cheaper than those from the Petite Champagne), and who wished to counter the highly effective Rémy publicity which emphasized the superiority of cognacs from the Champagnes. In the end the Big Three abandoned their initiative. The war, crucially, had divided the growers, those from the Champagnes setting up their own federation.

The growers were unprepared for the crisis which overtook the region in the 1970s. In the postwar euphoria production had greatly increased. As the table on page xx shows, although the area planted with vines remained below 110,000 hectares, less than half the area reached in the euphoric 1970s, yet viticultural techniques had so improved that by 1973 production reached twice the pre-phylloxera volume, the equivalent of 264 million bottles, over twice that year's sales. In 1973 came the oil shock; and although sales of cognac in France remained buoyant (until checked by a sharp tax increase in 1983) this helped only Martell and Courvoisier of the Big Four, since Rémy Martin and Hennessy depended upon exports for 95% of their sales.

The Chinese Market

They were saved largely by the increasing prosperity of the Chinese communities in Southeast Asia and their ability to satisfy the thirst for the fine, brown cognacs which they love to drink with meals. Hennessy had pioneered the trade, followed before World War II by Rémy Martin, and in the 1970s by all the other houses. Sales were also boosted by the growth of the American market. The acceptable, advertised, face of cognac in the USA was the after dinner consumption by the well-bred and well-heeled. The other, less-vaunted, boost was provided by the increased consumption of brandy by the black community in major cities such as Detroit and Cleveland. Only a handful of merchants (more especially Hennessy) had enough resources to tackle the American market; the relative stagnation of sales elsewhere badly affected many smaller merchants. By the early 1980s the Big Four controlled nearly four-fifths of exports, while the domestic market was cutthroat. There was no lack of foreign buyers for the faltering smaller firms. In 1986–87 alone, Bass, the English brewers, bought Otard, while Suntory, the Japanese distillers, bought Louis Royer.

Inevitably, during the difficult years, the major firms (even Rémy) had to cut back on their purchases from the growers. The European Economic Community assisted by paying growers, especially in the outlying areas, to pull up their vines – which will help to improve quality in the 1990s. However, the survivors often had to help themselves. The directory of Cognac firms is peppered with the names of growers who, for generations, had supplied major firms, and who found themselves partly or entirely abandoned in the 1970s. They went out to sell for themselves and began by selling directly to French customers, always anxious to have their own source of supply. Because only a few private customers buy cognacs by the case, the growers either toured France's innumerable country fairs, or sold to groups in factories and offices. Some went further afield and an increasing number of these single-vineyard cognacs are now available outside France, most conspicuously in Holland, West Germany and Britain.

Although the process of adjustment has been painful, the end result is a healthy one. For one of Cognac's major problems, ironically, has been the high standards set by Martell and Hennessy, and followed by Rémy Martin. There appeared to be little room for the small specialist firms and individual growers who are the glory of other French wine and spirit-making regions. Now these are beginning to emerge, and with them an increasing recognition of the individual qualities to be found in cognacs from specific areas and of different ages. In theory the search for individuality should favour the Champagnes. But – as explained on pages xx and xx – pockets of potential quality can be found in the Borderies, the Fins Bois and even in the Bons Bois, so there is now room for greater individuality in Cognac's offerings than ever before.

THE INGREDIENTS OF COGNAC

Geography

On an ordinary map the Cognac region is a small square tucked away in the French midwest. On closer examination it occupies a central position, for it is right on the frontier which traditionally divides northern from southern France, the point where, in the Middle Ages, the northern Langue d'Oil was replaced by the southern Langue d'Oc. Cognac is also midway between the sandy, marshy Biscay coast and the wooded uplands of the Massif Central.

The climate is equally central. Cognac is well south of the River Loire, traditionally the point where the weather loses its northern harshness and is replaced by a more temperate climate. It rarely freezes (the snow in early 1987 was the first for over a decade), and although the summers can be disagreeably hot and muggy in Cognac itself, they are not hot or dry enough to cause problems for the vines.

Climatically, as well as geographically, Cognac is on the great semicircular sweep running from Bordeaux north to the Loire, and then east to Champagne and Burgundy, which marks the northern limit of modern vine cultivation in France.

Because the quality of a fruit, and the intensity of its taste, depend on it suffering, on not being able to grow too lushly, this marginality is crucial to the quality of the grapes and consequently the wines and spirits produced by them. But the balance is a delicate one. Exposure to brisk sea breezes affects the quality of the spirits made on the broad coastal plain between Cognac and the Bay of Biscay, while to the east the weather grows more extreme, more Continental as one moves towards the foothills of the Massif Central. So, whatever the geological factors, the climate restricts the finest cognacs to a semicircle around Cognac and Jarnac. Equally, in Cognac, as elsewhere in temperate climates, the finest wines or spirits are made from grapes grown on hillsides. In Cognac these can be deceptively gentle and rolling, but the slopes exist none the less (although the aspect matters less than in many other northern grape-

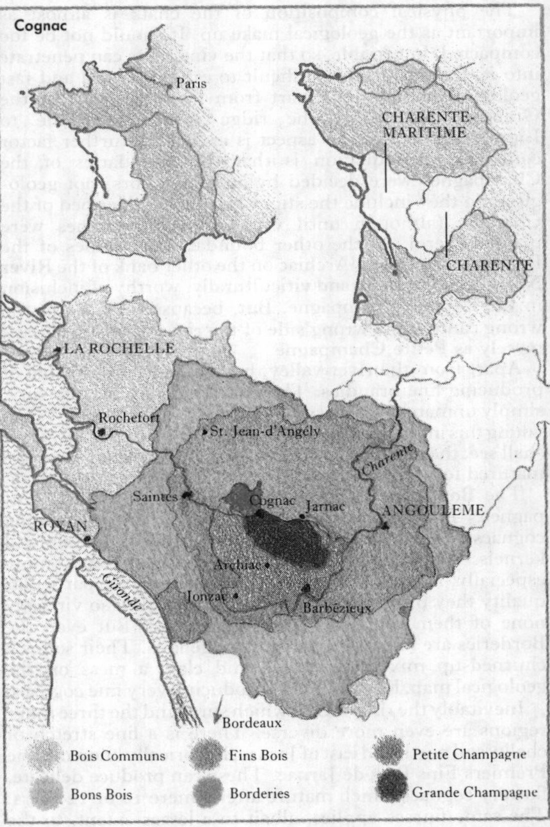

growing climates and only in cold years does a northern aspect seriously handicap the maturation of the grapes).

Geology

Despite the importance of the weather, geology is the crucial determinant of the quality of cognacs. The spirit's reputation rests solidly on chalk, and chalk of very particular varieties. The Grande Champagne, an irregular quadrilateral south of the Charente, is formed of chalks so particular that geologists have named them after the region. The crest of the rolling slopes of the Grande Champagne are composed of Campanian chalk, named after the Latin original of the word which became Champagne. Below them (and thus emerging lower down the slopes) is another unusual type of chalk, the Santonian, again named specially for the region (Saintonge), as is the Coniacian chalk found around Cognac. Another test of a slope's suitability for growing cognac is the concentration of a particular type of fossil, *Ostrea vesicularis*.

The physical composition of the chalk is almost as important as the geological make up. It should not be too compacted, but friable, so that the vine roots can penetrate into it. Because it is so difficult to establish hard and fast geological boundaries (apart from the very heart of the Grande Champagne, the ridge from Ambleville to Lignières) the physical aspect is crucial. A further factor confusing the equation is that the boundaries of the Champagnes were decided by administrators, not geologists. So they include the sticky clay of the river bed of the Charente (although until very recently no vines were planted there). At the other boundary, the slopes of the Petite Champagne d'Archiac on the other bank of the River Né, are, geologically and viticulturally, worthy of inclusion in the Grande Champagne. But, because they are in the wrong canton, the wrong side of the river, they are classed merely as Petite Champagne.

Apart from the river valley, both regions are capable of producing fine brandies. They have a depth, an intensity, simply unmatchable by any other spirit in the world. When young this intensity comes over as fiery harshness, but, as we shall see, the mysterious chemistry involved when a spirit is matured for decades in wood allows the depths to emerge.

The Borderies are even more special than the Champagnes. They are a small rectangle of land producing cognacs which have a most appealing nuttiness, like almond kernels. They are much used by Hennessy and, more especially, Martell, which refuse to abandon the particular quality they bring even to their best brandies (so virtually none of them can be called Champagne). But even the Borderies are not geologically homogenous. Their soil is a churned-up mixture of chalk and clay, a mess on the geological map, but capable of producing very fine cognacs.

Inevitably the ring of *Bois* which surround the three inner regions are even more diverse. There is a fine stretch of chalky soil north and east of Jarnac, historically known as the Premiers Fins Bois de Jarnac. These can produce delicate, flowery cognacs which mature after a mere 10 or 12 years. The same finesse applies, albeit to a lesser extent, to the relatively narrow eastern and southeastern belts of Fins Bois round Blanzac, and to the Fins Bois (and an irregular belt of chalky Bon Bois) to the south of Barbézieux. By no coincidence these are precisely the areas where one finds the biggest concentration, outside the Champagnes, of growers selling their products directly. They are also the zones where the buyers from the most reputable houses concentrate their purchases (very few look further than the Fins Bois, and those who do buy in the Bon Bois do so only to the south.

This leaves the great western belt of the region, which produces relatively ordinary cognacs. Unfortunately, the thinnest and sharpest, those produced on the islands off the coast, are the cognacs usually offered to the hundreds of thousands of tourists who throng the local beaches every summer. Fortunately – despite the tourist demand – a severe Darwinian selection process has thinned drastically the vines west of Cognac (the process started a century ago after the ravages of the phylloxera, when many farmers in marginal areas, especially in the north and west, turned to dairy farming, their pioneering cooperatives producing the famous Charentais butter).

Even though the soil becomes less chalky and more sandy as one moves towards the coast there are pockets of chalk in odd places, notably the upper estuary of the Gironde round St-Tomas-de-Conäc. Not surprisingly, a number of direct-selling growers have their vineyards in this pocket, although connoisseurs detect the iodiny, seaweedy, influence of the salt sea air in their products.

The Vines

Legally the Cognaçais may use a number of grape varieties, although the choice is largely theoretical. The Ugni Blanc accounts for over 90% of the total area. The rest is entirely Folle Blanche and Colombard. Not a single grower or firm mentioned any other variety when replying to our questionnaire. This concentration is directly attributable to phylloxera. Cognac's rise to fame was based upon two varieties, the Balzac and the Folle (later known as the Folle Blanche), both much despised by locals only interested in fine wines. In the 18th century the Colombard, which made the delicious sweet white wines from the Borderies, also rose to prominence. Judging by a pure Colombard sample tasted in California*, it ripens quickly to a kind of butterscotchy warmth but, crucially, finishes very short and does not, as do the best brandies, linger on the palate.

Folle Blanche was the raw material for the brandies which were the glory of Cognac's pre-phylloxera heyday. The wine it produced was so acid as to be virtually undrinkable, although this was no bar to producing a fine, aromatic cognac with an unmatched depth of flavour. Not unnaturally, the Folle Blanche is still remembered with affection. Tragically, when it was grafted onto American rootstocks, it flourished too vigorously. The bunches were so tightly packed that the grapes in the middle were liable to grey rot so pervasive that it could not be reached by antirot sprays.

So the Ugni Blanc triumphed. As the name implies, it was originally an Italian variety, the Trebbiano Toscano from the hills of the Emilia Romagna near Piacenza. It is now so widespread that, according to Jancis Robinson it probably produces more wine than any other variety. In France it is the most widely planted vine, helped by the almost 100,000 hectares devoted to it in the Charente. Its popularity is in marked contrast to its qualities. These are summed up, crisply but accurately by Jancis Robinson: "Pale lemon, little nose, notably high acid, medium alcohol and body, short. And that, I am afraid, is it. It is a very characterless wine indeed. As a vine, its twin virtues are the tenacity with which it keeps its acid right up to a late ripening . . . and, of course, its extraordinarily high yields"†. These two qualities make it an ideal variety for providing a suitably neutral, suitably acid base wine for cognac.

After the phylloxera the vines, which had previously been planted higgledy-piggledy, were planted in rows and replanted every 35 years. Until recently they were pruned back hard, but are now cultivated on trellises, between 1 and

* At the RMS distillery run by Rémy Martin, *see* Page 62.
† *Vines, Wines and Grapes*, Mitchell Beazley, 1986.

1.5 metres high, to make them easier to work by machines. For the same reason, they are planted relatively far apart, with about 2.8 metres between the rows. The hard pruning is designed to reduce yields but, thanks to improved viticultural techniques, these have risen sharply since 1945, reaching a maximum of the equivalent of over 3,000 bottles of cognac per hectare in 1973. New methods of cultivation have a major disadvantage: the grapes furthest from the ground can no longer catch the warmth reflected from the chalky soil and, therefore, ripen more slowly.

The Ugni Blanc is a southern vine and, even before the recent changes, the grapes did not ripen fully, even though they were not generally harvested until late October. Even so the wine they produce is weak and acid, varying between 7° and 10°. The grapes merely provide a base for distillation and the differences between individual years, so crucial elsewhere, do not matter greatly, since there are many other variables in the long chain between the grape harvest and the drinker. All that matters is healthy grapes. This obsession is natural enough, given the basic rule that the slightest impurity in the raw material is automatically multiplied in the distillation process.

The wine is invariably distilled to around 70° so, in theory, the weaker the wine, the more concentrated the flavour and the better the brandy. This is only partly true. In a hot summer the grapes run the risk of becoming (relatively) too rich and consequently the brandy is flabby – this was noticeable in 1976, when the grapes reached a natural 12°. Four years later, by contrast, the harvest was late, the grapes were almost frozen and their potential flavour largely neutralized by the cold. Similarly, grapes picked at below 7° are liable to be unsound, or even half-ripe. To be safe the Cognaçais like to harvest between 8° and 9°.

The Wine

The wine making is designed, not to provide a wine of quality, but an acceptable, pure, raw material. This is more difficult than it sounds. Before the wine can be distilled it has to undergo its malolactic fermentation, when the bitter malic acid is transformed into the more benevolent lactic acid. It does not matter if the wine has not undergone what the French call *le malo*, but it must not be distilled during the transformation.

It is more difficult to avoid the use of sulphur dioxide (SO_2), the disinfectant added, as a matter of routine, to all other white wines to prevent oxidation and deter bacteria. The yeasts and the SO_2 combine to produce a lot of aldehydes. The compound formed by the SO_2 and the aldehydes is stable in wine, but disintegrates when heated in a still. The resulting mixture gives off a smell of acetal, powerfully reminiscent of the disinfectants used in hospitals. Fortunately the need for SO_2 is removed because the wine is very acid and is distilled soon after fermentation.

Distillation

For the growers who now sell their own products their cognacs are the result of an integrated operation, the grapes grown, the wine made, the cognac distilled, aged and sold all in the same place. But this is the exception. Most of them also sell some cognac to the major firms. Some of these have vineyards of their own and most have substantial distilleries, largely using bought-in wines. But none supply more than half their requirements because most of the wine is distilled either by the handful of *bouilleurs de profession*, who act merely as distillers for the growers and merchants, or by the thousands of *bouilleurs de crus*; growers with their own stills. Their role and status vary widely. A few hundred sell some of their own production, but the vast majority of the 25,000 *bouilleurs* have some form of contract to sell some or all of their brandy, either newly distilled or after a year or even ten in cask, to the blender who will sell the final product. In many cases the style of the brandy produced is dictated by the requirements of the firm to which they are under contract.

All the distillers operate under the same strict rules. The wine has to be distilled twice to a maximum strength of 72°; the stills have to be of the historic shape; the vat must be made of copper – the only truly neutral metal, guaranteed not to react with the boiling liquid – and heated by a naked external flame.

Although the still used for the first distillation may hold up to 130 hectolitres, that used for the *bonne chauffe*, the second distillation, may not hold more than 30 hectolitres, nor be filled with more than 25 hectolitres of liquid. Distillation starts in late November, a mere month after the usual date for the harvest, and continues until the spring. Obviously the sooner the wine is distilled the better. The raw material is fresher, and if the distillation is left until the spring the absence of sulphur may begin to tell on its purity. There is also the danger that it may start to referment (cognacs distilled after 31 March following the harvest lose a year of their age. *See* the rules on page 34).

The basic design of the *alembic charentais* was perfected by the Dutch in the 17th century and it has not changed greatly since then. It is designed to provide a steady flow of alcohol released gently by heating the wine to about 600°C. In effect the wine is made to evaporate, and its essences removed as tenderly as possible. In the days when the stills were heated by wood, or even by coal, providing a steady, gentle, adjustable flame was a major problem. However, since the 1950s natural gas from the field at Lacq in the Pyrenees has solved the problem of providing clean, reliable, controllable fuel.

The bulbous onion-shaped vat (*cucurbite*) in which the wine is boiled is surmounted by a smaller chamber, of the same shape, called the *chapiteau* (literally the big top, or circus tent). The *chapiteau* should be only one-tenth the size of the *alembic* (still); the combination resembles an old-fashioned cottage loaf or the double dome of a Russian Orthodox church. The *chapiteau* traps the alcoholic vapours which are then led down a *bec* (beak) to a *serpentin*, a condenser or cooling coil, from which the liquid – the condensate – drips into a double-bottomed pail (*bassiot*).

Despite the standardization, the distiller has a number of choices which bear on the quality of the final product. Growing grapes to make wine for cognac may be a routine,

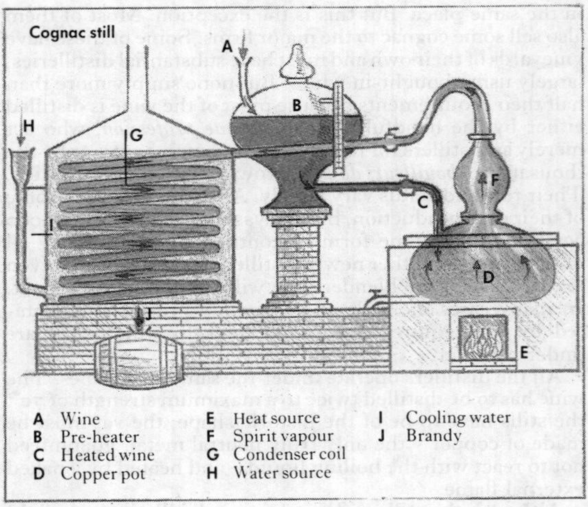

quasi-industrial process, but the art of making cognac starts with distillation. The choices mainly relate to the design of the still. The first variable is simply its size. The smaller the still, the more distinctive the brandy produced; the bigger it is, the more neutral the flavour (originally the stills held a mere three hectolitres; some older ones in use today often hold 10 hectolitres or less, under half that held in the standard modern still). The same applies to the *chapiteau*; the bigger it is in relation to the still the more effectively it rectifies the spirit.

The shape of the *bec* has also changed. The original *bec* was called a *tête de Maure* (Moor's Head), and was an angular affair. The modern *bec* is infinitely smoother and more rounded, as the name *col de cygne* (swan's neck) implies. The height of the *col de cygne* inevitably increases the degree of rectification and contributes to ensure that modern cognac is almost certainly smoother, less characterful, than it was even before 1914.

The distiller's next choice is whether to use a *chauffe-vin*, a simple tub in which the warmth of the hot vapour is used to preheat the wine waiting to be distilled. This sharply reduces fuel costs. Its supporters claim that the use of such a heat exchanger is merely a physical process, although they do admit that if the wine is preheated to more than 40°C it may become oxidized; this danger is increased should the pipes become blocked, which is why Martell will not use a *chauffe-vin*. For them purity is more important than reduced fuel bills.

Distillers also disagree over whether or not the wine should be distilled on its lees to extract as much fruitiness from the grape as possible. Rémy Martin hastens the maturation of brandies from the Champagnes by distilling the wines on their lees, as do some of the most conscientious growers. This is reasonable enough. The yeasts in the lees contain a number of esters which provide an increased richness to the flavour. The same motive determines the time the liquid is heated, which can vary between eight and 12 hours. As one might expect, the slower the cooking, the more thoroughly the essential qualities of the fruit are extracted. At an initial glance it would appear that the first *chauffe*, which concentrates the wine three or four times, to produce a *brouillis* between 26 and 32%, is less important than the second, known as the *bonne chauffe*, which produces the cognac itself. But this is not the case. Although the *brouillis* is undrinkable, and impossible even for the distiller to judge, most of the vital chemical reactions take place when the liquid is first heated.

The distinctions between different cognacs can be increased by varying the cutoff points in the second *chauffe*. In the first the cutoffs are automatic. The first vapours, at around 55%, are both too strong and too clogged with impurities picked up in the *serpentin* to be usable. The flow is cut off when the vapour, at around 5%, is too weak to be useful. At the start of the *bonne chauffe* the first half per cent or so is equally mucky and is diverted. The liquid must be clear; but the decision when to allow the liquid through to the cask is not based on its physical properties alone. Obviously it must be clear, but if, like Martell, one is looking for a relatively neutral base spirit the early vapours are allowed through, even though they may be too strong for many cognac styles. The final cutoff point, when the *secondes* are set to one side, is even more important. It can be cut off early to produce a relatively neutral style, if (like Martell) that is the requirement, or the cognacs are to be matured for a couple of decades to acquire their character from the wooden casks. If (like Bisquit) one wants to extract the maximum fruitiness, at the risk of including some rather acrid elements, the cutoff is late, at 67% or below. The range is a mere 3%, the parameters between 67° and 72°, but the potential stylistic difference is enormous.

There is yet one final, non-scientific, decision to be made. If the *secondes* set to one side are mixed with the wine waiting for the *première chauffe*, the raw material is stronger and the final spirit more neutral (since some of the wine will have been distilled four times). If the *secondes* are mixed with the *brouillis*, the brandies are more aromatic, benefiting from the maximum fruitiness of the original grapes.

Oak and Maturation

Cognac would never have achieved its fame had it not been situated down river from and with immediate access to the wood from the oak forests of the Limousin, east of Angoulême. Oak casks play a double role in the creation of cognac. Newly distilled cognac is merely an intermediate product; its final qualities depending critically upon the chemical reactions of the brandy with wood and air (oxygen).

This is recognized by the major firms who dread the loss of quality (and of cognac) resulting from imperfect casks. Martell has a major cooperage of its own. Hennessy and Rémy Martin (since 1945) have bought up two of the biggest cask makers in France, Taransaud and Séguin-Moreau.

Both sell a substantial proportion of their output to other customers in France and California. Recently Hennessy even bought its own oak forest.

Physically oak is tough, watertight and not too porous, yet supple enough to be worked into casks. Its chemical constituents are even more important. Fortunately none are negative, for oak contains few of the resins which would give the brandy an unpleasantly resinous taste. The cellulose, which comprises 70% of the wood, absorbs some of the sugars in the course of maturation – although its role is principally physical, providing the wood with its strength. The single most important component is probably the lignin which comprises about 23% of the wood. The lignin imparts an agreeable aroma of balsam, and when its molecules break down they produce the vanilla and cinnamon overtones which make some older brandies so memorable. The lignin is more important than the better known tannins, which account for only 5% of the wood. Tannins, however, add colour to the originally colourless cognac; and although at first they impart a bitter taste, with age they mellow the tannins in the brandy as they do those in red wines.

Limousin and Tronçais

The Limousin has always been a natural forest, where the trees have room to grow large and thick. The wood is relatively porous, with more tannin than the other oak used in Cognac today, from the man-made forest of the Tronçais in the very centre of France, just west of Burgundy. The Tronçais forest was planted on the orders of the great 17th century French statesman, Colbert, to provide wood for the French navy so that it could compete with the British men-of-war and their famous "hearts of oak". The trees in Tronçais are planted close together, so they grow tall and narrow, their wood tighter packed than the free-range wood from the Limousin. Tronçais oak, with less tannin and more lignin than its rival, is ideal for shorter periods of maturation since the cognacs absorb less tannin than in Limousin.

The timber used is carefully chosen. The staves must be free from knots or other imperfections and are sawn only from the trunks of trees which are at least 50 years old. It also has to be dried, legally for at least three years, in fact for at least five. Drying in the open air is important because the wind and the rain wash away the more bitter of the tannins. The actual making of the casks is a fascinating process which can never be fully mechanized. Visiting a cooperage is an unforgettable experience; the aromas from the wood being sawn and shaped and charred are enhanced by the flames from the flickering fires used to bend the emerging staves.

In theory all cognac is housed exclusively in the classic cognac casks made in these cooperages. Originally these casks held a mere 205 litres, a size which increased the intensity and woodiness of the cognacs. But the best size, found by trial and error, for combining maturation and porosity, is 350 litres; this is the size of cask shown to visitors. Almost every respondent to our enquiries admitted that he also held a quantity of cognac in larger *tonneaux*. Many of these are used simply for blending, or for housing the *petites eaux* which dilute the cognac before it is sold. Not all cognac is scrupulously housed for its whole life in the classic *barriques*, and in large casks it has not nearly as much access to the wood, or oxygen in the air, as if it were housed in smaller containers.

As the section on legal definitions on page xxx shows, there are lower age limits at which firms can market their cognacs, although this applies only to the ordinary qualities. The BNIC admits defeat when it comes to keeping track of the exact age of cognacs more than six years old. After that stage one has to rely on the palate and, more reliably, the reputation of the firm selling the cognac.

All cognacs have a "learning curve". Their quality rises with time and then, after a certain point, the curve flattens and the maturation process slows down and stops. The curves obviously vary for brandies from the different *crus*. Those from the outer ring, the Bois Ordinaires, virtually all the Bons Bois and some of the Fins Bois to the west of Cognac, are not going to acquire any depth or complexity however long and lovingly they are stored. They will be drinkable after their fourth birthday (few reputable firms sell blends which contain any brandies less than a year above the legal minimum age of two and a half years).

Nothing in Cognac is more confusing than the many names firms employ to describe their different offerings. These divide into four or five bands. VS or ☆☆☆ is almost invariably less than five years old: VSOP between five and 10, although firms are allowed to call their blends VSOP even if the average age is five or six, generally too young for other than the most basic cognac. Rémy Martin's minimum of seven years for its VSOP, the biggest seller of that quality in the world, should be a bench mark (especially as the firm prides itself on the techniques used to speed the maturation of cognacs from the Champagnes). Then comes the intermediate range, usually called Napoléon, between seven and 15 years old. The best "ordinary" cognacs, the XOs (including Martell's Cordon Bleu) are fine cognacs of over 20 years of age when all the *crus* have had the time to reach their best.

Remember that these names can mean almost anything. A reputable firm will use brandies far older than required by the law, and of course the age refers only to the youngest brandy in a blend; the average should be much higher.

The individual growers who sell their own cognacs from the Fins Bois offer their best products at about 15 years of age. They get noticeably finer and more elegant in the years after their tenth birthday, but no one thinks it worth his while to keep them longer than 20 years. The Borderies are another matter. The Rothschilds of Château Lafite sell a genuinely old Borderies, reckoned to be up to 50 years old. It is a little too richly woody for my taste, but it makes the point; the inherent nuttiness and warmth of these cognacs are increased by a couple of decades in cask.

Cognacs from the Champagnes can be sold young; the quality of Rémy's VSOP proves that. It is only towards the end of their second decade in cask that the tannin softens to develop another dimension – the famous *rancio*, the cheesy richness much prized by some connoisseurs. It takes another two decades for the whole mixture to mature, so that by its fortieth birthday the curve has flattened and, to my palate (and that of some of the blenders) the brandy is as good as it will ever be. It combines the warmth, the depth, the fruitiness, the complexity of a great spirit.

The tiny minority of brandies which remain in cask after their fortieth birthday are soon transferred to massive glass jars (*bonbonnes*) holding 25 litres. The glass is neutral; the brandies have no further access to the air; they remain embalmed. Curiously, age confers a sort of anonymity upon these cognacs. They can be quite extraordinary, but the oldest blends on the market – eg. Rémy Martin's Louis XIII and Hennessy's Paradis – are less distinctive than their younger XOs.

While the age of a cognac is crucial, the balance between new and old oak casks, and the length of time spent in new oak, also plays a major role in the final result. Obviously old casks are more neutral, they have already lost much of their tannin and have less to transmit to the brandy. Most houses keep their better cognacs in new wood for between six and nine months. The major exceptions both come from the Grande Champagne, from Delamain, and the Château de Fontpinot, an estate between Ambleville and Lignières, marketed by the Cointreau family, which also owns the firm of Frapin. Delamain buys its brandies from suppliers who never use any new wood; Frapin keeps the brandies from Fontpinot in new wood for up to two years. These would be undrinkable unless kept for at least another decade to soften the strong dose of tannin received from the new wood. Delamain's cognacs rely exclusively on their inherent depth and fruitiness, and emerge as more delicate and elegant than those from Fontpinot which, reinforced by a strong dose of tannin, are inevitably more robust. Choosing between them is largely a matter of personal preference.

Storage

As important as the type of wood are the conditions of storage. The Cognaçais benefited from their riverside site, not only to transport their wares, but also to provide damp storage conditions. The more humid the cellar, the greater the loss of alcoholic strength in a given period. Cognacs stored in drier conditions, therefore, will be harsher, and stronger. The firms are fully aware of this fact. When Bisquit moved its cellars from the riverside at Jarnac to a hill top 20 miles away it deliberately used air conditioning to recreate the atmosphere of the original cellarage.

Damp cellars, plus old wood, were two of the conditions which created the English aristocratic tradition still exemplified by Delamain and Hine. Nevertheless the tradition, like so many others, is a late 19th century invention. Until then the British, like the Chinese today, tended to prefer their brandies warm and brown, so the firms responded by adding generous doses of caramel. But this somehow became thought of as rather vulgar. Eventually they were replaced (among the classier buyers anyway) by more elegant cognacs described as "early-landed, late-bottled". They were shipped a year or so after distillation, stored in dockside warehouses in Bristol, London or Leith (the port for Edinburgh) and then sold under the importer's name.

The tradition is still maintained by a number of British merchants. It carries with it another major advantage. French regulations forbid the Cognaçais from putting a precise date on their labels. If a cognac is shipped immediately after distillation and stored in a bonded warehouse until it is bottled decades later, the customs documents provide sufficient proof that it came from a specific vintage. (Unfortunately some of the casks were moved to drier cellars when the London docks were abandoned, and a number of firms are faced with the problem of far harsher and stronger cognacs than they – or their customers – anticipated.)

British importers deal with single lots of cognac. Traditionally cognac has always been a blend and the secret of the house styles, described in the next section, consists, not only in the types of cognac, the wood used, and the ages of the brandies in the blend, but in the personal vision of the firm's owner or his blender. It is usually a vision related to the market but some blenders (like Alain Braastad at Delamain) feel free to blend the cognacs to their personal taste.

They all, however, have common problems when preparing their brandies for market. These now have to be brought down to strength, and the blender has to decide which, if any, additives are required. Cognac starts its life at 67 to 70% and is sold at 40%, a strength it will reach if left in cask for 35 to 50 years. Some small firms sell part of their older cognacs at their natural strength (which makes them more expensive, since duties are proportional to the alcohol).

The vast majority of cognacs have to be diluted; and the younger they are sold, the stronger they are and the greater the dilution required. The process is a gradual one. No reputable blender would add the required quantity of diluent at one time, or just before the cognac was to be bottled. Normally six months to five years are left for the process. Distilled water is used, but some of the most scrupulous use *petites eaux*, weak brandy-and-water.

The blenders are relatively open about the speed with which they reduce their brandies to saleable strength, and surprisingly frank about the other three additives which are allowed: one part caramel per thousand to standardize the colour; up to eight grams sugar per litre to soften the blend; and *boisé*, oak chips soaked in old cognac, to provide a false impression of additional age.

The use of caramel is the result of the Cognaçais' desire to standardize their product and has no perceptible effect upon the taste – although a few purists refuse to add it; part of a trend against additives of any description. Otherwise there seems to be a general, tacit, agreement that caramel and sugar syrup are both natural. Typical is Jean-Luc Pasquet of Eraville (like most of the growers quoted here he is based in a favoured corner of the Champagnes). He is conscientious enough to reduce the strength of his cognacs by adding water drop by drop over a period of three years, but adds 0.3% of sugar syrup and 1% of caramel: "for reasons of homogeneity". Paul Giraud of Bouteville prides himself on the humidity of his cellars, the length of time his brandies spend there and the natural sweetness they acquire. He eschews *boisé* – and to preserve their natural colour does without caramel. Nevertheless he adds ¾% of sugar syrup.

Caramel and sugar syrup are added during the blending process or – and the two usually go together – when the cognac is being diluted. In other words the two additives can be thought of as finishing touches, and not fundamental to the cognac itself. *Boisé* is another matter. It is usually added to cognac within the first two years of its life in an attempt to speed the apparent age of the brandy; to give the impression that it is older than it is. *Boisé* is also useful because it compensates for any lack of character in cognacs left in large casks for most of their maturation period. Very few of our respondents were as honest as Guy Testaud of Lamerac, who adds caramel and *boisé* when his VSOP and Napoléon qualities are two years old: "to try and age them artificially". Paul Bonnin of Challignac, near Barbézieux, adds *boisé* when the cognacs are young: "to improve the age of the cognac". M. Clair of Archiac uses 2% of *boisé*: "to increase the sweetness". M. Forgeron of Segonzac adds ½% to his younger cognacs: "to compensate for the lack of tannin in the older casks or tonneaux".

The concern for standardization reflected in the widespread use of caramel has been very useful for the Cognaçais in the majority of markets. It is one reason why sales of their spirits are 10 times that of the Armagnaçais, their only rivals in the quality stakes. During the past 20 years their rivals have captured the commanding heights of quality within France itself, using two weapons: dating their brandies, and pin-pointing the source to an individual estate, usually attached to the name of a château or domaine. The Cognaçais cannot put a date on their cognacs; the use of the word château or domaine is forbidden unless the cognac originates from a specific place. Because cognac is such big business, and growers could sell their output so easily, and at increasing prices until 1973, there was no incentive for originality. Now, at a time of seemingly permanent surplus, when even the biggest houses are cutting down on their purchases, individual growers are increasingly aware of the value placed by discerning (or merely snobby) buyers upon any product bearing the mark of a specific person or place of origin, as the French put it, *artisanale*. Given the distinctive individual qualities available from many favoured spots scattered over the Cognac region, this trend is both welcome and likely to accelerate. In the past the high quality of the brandies sold by Martell and Hennessy has been both a blessing and a curse. A blessing because it was important for Cognac that the two firms which accounted for 40% of the market should project an image of quality; a curse because their quality seemingly left less room for specialists. Rémy Martin pioneered an alternative route with its insistence upon the quality of its brandies from the Champagnes. Its successors are a host of individual growers, proud, not of their *cru* so much as the specific qualities of their patch of earth as reflected in their wares. Vive la difference!

The Legal Definition of Cognac

Cognac is governed by the Bureau National Interprofessionel du Cognac (BNIC), representing all the interested parties, including a Commissaire du Gouvernement. It both issues and administers the regulations covering the production, distillation, ageing and sale of cognac and collects the statistics relating to the production of wine and cognac.

The term "cognac" may be used only of spirits made from grapes grown, fermented and distilled in the region as defined on the map on page 23, which also defines the sub-appellations: Grande Champagne, Petite Champagne, Borderies, Fins Bois, Bons Bois.

The word "fine" may be added to any such description but the words "Fine Champagne" may be used only of spirit coming entirely from the Champagnes, with at least 50% from the Grande Champagne. Descriptions such as "clos", "château" or "domaine" implying that the spirit comes from a specific geographical spot may be used only with the permission of the BNIC.

The principal grape varieties permitted are the Folle Blanche, St Emilion-des-Charentes (also known as the Ugni Blanc) and the Colombard. Five other varieties can, in theory, be used for up to 10% of the total, but none are actually grown.

Wine making must be conducted as by local custom. Continuous Archimedes presses, and the addition of sugar to the must are both specifically prohibited. Cognac may travel on the public highway only when accompanied by a gold-coloured transport certificate (*Acquit Jaune d'Or*).

The spirit must be distilled twice, to a final strength not exceeding 72%. The *alembic* used for the first distillation can hold up to 130 hectolitres: those used for the second distillation must not hold more than 30 hectolitres, nor be charged with more than 25 hectolitres.

Before sale cognac must be reduced to between 40 and 45% alcohol through the addition of distilled water or weaker spirit (*petites eaux*) which must also come from the Cognac region. Additives are limited to caramel, sugar, and oak chips. Up to 2% sugar may be added, either in the form of syrup or sugar soaked in spirit of 20 to 30%. Colouring matter is limited to two parts per thousand.

All cognacs are registered by age – ageing officially starts on 31 March each year.

Compte 00: cognacs distilled between the harvest and the following 31 March, at which point they turn into *Compte* 0 cognacs. Brandies distilled after 1 April retain their 00 designation until the following 31 March.

Compte 1: cognacs more than 1 year old on 1 April of a given year.

Comptes 2, 3, 4 and 5: cognacs from two to five years old on 1 April.

Compte 6: cognacs more than six years old.

Cognacs may not be sold in France until they are at least *Compte* 2. These can be called only VS or ☆☆☆ – other countries (including Britain, Ireland, Malaysia, Hong Kong, South Korea and New Zealand) demand a minimum age of three years.

To be called Réserve, VO or VSOP, the youngest brandy in the blend must be at least 4½ years old (ie. *Compte* 4).

To be labelled Extra, Napoléon, Vieux, Vieille Réserve etc., the youngest spirit in the blend must be at least *Compte* 6.

No official regulations cover cognacs older than *Compte* 6.

COGNAC

· DIRECTORY ·

This list is limited to firms which sell their cognacs outside the region. The numbers which follow the types of cognac indicate the ages claimed by the firms. All the cognacs are sold at 40° unless otherwise stated. Most firms welcome visitors by appointment. Opening hours given are only for those which run organized tours. Cognacs coming from specific subregions are indicated as follows:

GC Grande Champagne
PC Petite Champagne
FC Fine Champagne (at least half Grande, the rest Petite Champagne)
B Borderies
FB Fins Bois
BB Bons Bois

Apart from Fine Champagne, the word Fine on a cognac bottle is meaningless and I have therefore ignored it.

ANSAC

See Unicognac.

AUGIER

Place de la Salle Verte, 16102 Cognac
Tel: (45) 82 00 01

The oldest firm in Cognac. Founded in 1643. In 1968 it was sold to Seagram and is now a mere shell.

BALLUET

J. Balluet, Neuvicq-le-Château, 17490 Beauvais-sur-Matha ***Tel: (46) 26 64 74***
Fine Cognac VSOP 8 · Cognac Très Vieille Réserve 20

Typical old-established grower. Since 1845 the family has been distilling the wines from its 35 hectares in the Fins Bois, relying exclusively on the product from its two stills, one modern, the other a tiny historic affair holding a mere 300 litres of wine.

The firm keeps its brandies for a considerable time, partly in classic small casks, some in larger casks. Within France Balluet sells only to private individuals, but exports to Britain, Belgium and West Germany. The premises command a splendid view of Cognac.

MICHEL BARLAAM

"Les Landes", Rioux Martin, 16210 Chalais
Tel: (45) 98 17 75
Michel Barlaam 10+ · Michel Barlaam VSOP 2+

M. Barlaam relies totally on the 12 hectares he owns in the Bons Bois, seven of them devoted to Ugni Blanc grapes for cognac. He has a substantial (15 hectolitre) 10-year-old still. 90% of his output is sold to private clients in France, the rest in West Germany, Britain and Belgium. He also prides himself on keeping his brandies for longer than the legal minimum.

MADAME GABRIEL DE BELLABRE

Philippe Lajoumard de Bellabré, L'Essart, La Chapelle des Pots, 17100 Saintes ***Tel: (46) 91 54 56***
Vieille Réserve (FB) 55° 12

M. Bellabré sells only one cognac, a 12-year-old Fins Bois at the natural strength (after 12 years in cask) of 55°.

JEAN BERGIER

Brivée-sur-Charente, 17800 Pons ***Tel: (46) 96 40 73***
VSOP (PC) 8 · Vieille Réserve (PC) 18–20

Small family grower, which has been selling only brandies from its 12 hectares of vines in the Petite Champagne since 1842. Relatively new 14 hectolitre still, some small Limousin oak casks, some more substantial tonneaux. Jean Bergier prides itself on the character of its VSOP provided by the age, and on the "subtle finesse and bouquet" of its Vieille Réserve.

BISQUIT

Société Ricard, Domaine de Lignières, 16170 Rouillac ***Tel: (45) 21 88 88***
XXX 3–5 · VSOP 8–10 · Napoléon 20–25 · Extra Vieille 50+ · Privilège d'Alexandre Bisquit 100

Tours in summer at 10 a.m., 3 p.m. and 4.30 p.m.

Established in Jarnac in 1819 by an enterprising local Alexandre Bisquit when he was only 20, after he had already started a business trading in the region's oldest staple product – salt. A staunch Republican, he was Mayor of Jarnac for a short time after the revolution of 1848. His daughter married Adrien Dubouché, who added his name to the firm. Their daughter married Maurice Laporte, a notable local figure who became a senator. But he was also active in the business, increasing sales especially to China and the Far East.

In 1965 the family sold the business to Paul Ricard, owner of Ricard Pastis. He also bought Château Lignières in the Fins Bois, near Rouillac, 20 miles northeast of Cognac. The estate, with 200 hectares of land, is the biggest in the Cognac region. M. Ricard planted it all with vines. But its grapes account for only between 12 and 18% of the firm's requirements. He also moved the firm's distillery and cellars from their historic site next to Hine on the river at Jarnac to Lignières where he built the biggest distillery in the region, an enormous modern installation holding 64 stills. The new warehouses are equipped with vast stacks with each cask lodged in its own "cell" so it can be moved separately by fork-lift truck. The premises are carefully insulated and the humidity controlled to ensure that the brandy matures at the same rate it did by the Charente.

Bisquit aims at a very fruity style of cognac and is prepared to accept more of the *secondes* than most other firms in order to retain as much of the fruit as possible. This is essential to give a young cognac some character which makes Bisquit XXX a much more satisfying brandy than most of its competitors.

PAUL BOCUSE

See Polignac.

DANIEL BOUJU

Lafont de St Preuil, 16130 Segonzac
Tel: (45) 83 41 27
XXX (GC) 4 · VSOP (GC) 7 · Napoléon (GC) 10 · Empereur (GC) 15 · Extra (GC) 25 · Très Vieux (GC) 32

The Bouju family has grown grapes at Segonzac, in the heart of the Grande Champagne, since 1805 and it still sells only what it produces on its 20 hectare holding. Bouju is very proud of its small still and that its cognacs are an absolutely pure product, unblended, without any additives. Daniel Bouju does not believe in market research, yet 85% of his production is sold outside France, all of it to restaurants and specialized outlets.

BOURON

SA Château de La Grange, BP 80, 17400 Saint Jean D'Angely ***Tel: (46) 32 00 12*** **and in Paris** ***(1 43) 06 49 97***
Bouron:
VSOP 10 (average) · Blason d'Or 15 (average) · Grande Réserve 30 (average) · Très Vieille Réserve 40 (average) · Réserve personnelle Limitée
Bouron/Maxim's de Paris:
VSOP 10 (average) · Napoléon 25 (average) · XO 35+

Housed in one of the region's most picturesque relics, the Château de la Grange, which dates back to the 13th century, once visited by King Louis XIII. The Bouron family has sold brandy since 1832, but only moved to the château in 1867. It now owns 90 hectares of vines, 40 each in the Borderies and the Petite Champagne, and 10 in the Fins Bois – although all the wine and cognac is made, and the cognac aged, at the château itself. It houses 10 stills of 25 hectolitres each, installed after 1945, as well as 1,500 Limousin oak casks of up to 400 litres.

Until recently the family sold all its cognacs for blending, but lately M. Bernard Parias and his wife Monique (née Bouron) have sold under their own name, mostly abroad in West Germany, Japan, the USA and South Korea. Under the Maxim label, as well as its own, it now sells to specialized outlets in France. All the cognacs are made from the family's own grapes: unusually none, not even the most expensive, are made purely from the Champagnes; and all are aged for longer than the legal minimum.

PIERRE BOUTINET

Bernard Boutinet, Le Bissonneau, Breville, 16370 Cherves de Cognac ***Tel: (45) 80 86 63***
Fine (FB) VSOP 6 · Vieille Fine Fins Bois (Napoléon) 12–14

A property of 26 hectares north of Cognac in a good region of the Fins Bois, owned by the same family for several generations. It is proud of being one of the rare growers which sells directly cognacs purely from the Fins Bois. M. Boutinet claims that his Fine Fins Bois is the equivalent of a VSOP, "golden colour, supple but firm in the mouth, long and powerful at the finish". He claims that his Vieille Fine

Fins Bois resembles a Napoléon in quality. It is darker, with some vanilla on the nose, full and long.

BOUTELLEAU

Once owned by the family of the writer Jacques Chardonne, who changed his name from Boutelleau. *See* Tiffon.

J. R. BRILLET

"Les Aireaux" Graves, 16120 Châteauneuf Charente, BP 37 *Tel: (45) 97 05 06*
Selection (PC) 3/4 · Grande Réserve (PC) 6/7 · Napoléon (FC) 10 · Hors d'Age (FC) 15–20 · Très Rare Heritage 45° 35–40 · Très Rare Réserve Limitée 80

The Brillet family has owned vines in the Grande and Petite Champagne since the 17th century and in 1850 set themselves up in a property in Graves. Run today by Jean Louis Brillet who relies mostly on the grapes from the family's 80 hectares of vines in the two Champagnes – although he does buy in some brandies varying from three to 80 years of age.

It distils the wines on the lees in its four stills to provide additional fruitiness. Honest in admitting that it adds a very little *boisé* to its Selection (recommended as particularly suitable for cognac cocktails) in its first months in cask to provide some balance. Particularly proud of its older cognacs: the Heritage is sold (in antique-style bottles) at the natural strength reached after 30 years in cask.

BRUGEROLLE

Cognac Brugerolle, 17160 Matha *Tel: (46) 58 50 60*
XXX 3–4 · VSOP 6–7 · Napoléon Aigle Rouge 10–12 · XO Napoléon Aigle d'Or 15–20 · Très Vieux Réserve 25–30

A typical small family business originally established in 1812 by a M. Jean Cornet from the Auvergne. Eighteen years later he was joined by a relative, M. Jean Brugerolle, and the firm is still run by the descendants of his nephew Etienne. The venerable figure of M. André Brugerolle, mayor of Matha for 30 years and a Member of the National Assembly for 20, presides over the firm which is now run by his son François and grandson Claude.

The family – though not the firm – owns vineyards and although it owns four stills they are all historic relics, 130 years old. So most of its cognacs are bought from a range of growers in the Fins Bois, the Bons Bois and the Champagnes. These are kept in casks of varying sizes. Its cognacs have wide foreign sales – indeed the Aigle Rouge brand was specially developed for Thailand.

CAMUS

Camus "La Grande Marque", 29 Rue Marguerite de Navarre, B.P. 19 16101 Cognac
Tel: (45) 32 28 28
Célébration · Napoléon · XO
Visits in summer.

Cognac's fifth largest firm and the biggest still in the hands of an individual family with total sales of FF350 million, 87% outside France. Founded in 1863 as La Grande Marquis, a consortium of growers headed by Jean-Baptiste Camus, who added his name to that of the group before his death in 1898. Camus depended largely on sales to Russia, and was the exclusive supplier to the Tsar. Inevitably it was badly affected by the Russian Revolution. It then aimed its sales to restaurants in bottle rather than, as previously, in cask.

Its present status is due to the late Michel Camus, grandson of the founder, who took over in 1934 at the age of 23. After 1945 the firm was in a bad way, but in the 1960s M. Camus was the only Cognaçais prepared to advance credit to two young Americans who held the concession for duty-free sales at Hong Kong Airport. Their firm, Duty-Free Shoppers, now controls these outlets all round the Pacific, remaining loyal to Camus, especially to the Célébration brand introduced particularly for duty-free shops.

Michel Camus also rebuilt the family's trade with Russia (the firm still owns the exclusive rights to market Russian vodka in France). He bought two important brands of armagnac, and his two sons have worthily maintained the family tradition since their father's death in 1985.

The family still owns 100 hectares of vines, notably at the Château d'Uffaut (just outside Cognac), at Bonneuil in Grande Champagne, at Vignolles and the Château de Plessis in the Borderies. These provide a mere 8% of the firm's requirements. Camus, as a family business, has never had the financial resources to hold as much stock as its competitors. It relies to a great extent on purchases of mature cognacs from growers and wholesalers in the Grande Champagne, the Borderies and the Fins Bois and Bons Bois.

CASTELBAJAC

See Logis de la Montagne.

CASTEL-SABLONS

Le Bourg, 17520 St Maigrin ***Tel: (46) 70 00 30***
Crystal Dry (FB) 3 · VSOP (FB) 8 · Napoléon (FB) 15

The Roux family owns 26 hectares in a favoured part of the Fins Bois, just south of the Petite Champagne. It has sold direct since 1976 and is on the look out for new products. Its young and virtually colourless Crystal Dry is deliberately designed as a base for cocktails. Its fearsome sounding Brûlot Charentais is a strong (58°) local firewater allegedly drunk at weddings, christenings and other festivities.

CASTILLON-RENAULT

See Renault.

GOURRY DE CHADEVILLE

16130 Segonzac ***Tel: (45) 83 40 54***
VSOP (GC) 5 · Napoléon (GC) 10–12 · Très Vieux (GC) 18–20

The Chadeville estate in the heart of the Grande Champagne has been owned by the Gourry family since 1619.

CLAUDE CHARAUD

St Leger, 17800 Pons ***Tel: (46) 96 90 77***
XXX (FB) 3 · VSOP (FB) 6 · VR (FB) 18

A classic small grower who has been selling his own cognac,

almost entirely to a private French clientele from a 10 hectare estate in the Fins Bois, for the past 20 years.

BERNARD CHARDEVOINES

Expiremont, 17130 Montendre ***Tel: (46) 49 21 29***
XXX (FB) 45° 5 · VSOP (FB) 45° 10 · Fine Cognac (FB) 45° 15

Small family holding of 14 hectares, 12 devoted to Ugni Blanc, in the unfashionable Bons Bois between Cognac and the Gironde. The Chardevoines started as a young couple, while in their twenties, with a tiny still in 1962, installing one of 18 hectolitres in the mid-1970s. In 1980 they started bottling their cognac themselves. They harvest their grapes by hand and sell their cognacs at their natural 45°.

CHATEAU DE BEAULON

Christian Thomas, Château de Beaulon, 17240 Saint Dizant du Gua ***Tel: (46) 49 96 13***
XXX 7 · VSOP 10 · Napoléon 20+ · Grande Fine Extra 40+

Cognac's most passionately ecological distiller, based on an historic estate once owned by the Bishop of Bordeaux, where the grapes have been distilled since 1712. Christian Thomas owns 90 hectares in the curious pocket of pure chalk on the banks of the Gironde. To improve quality he has retained a proportion of Folle Blanche and Colombard vines; he uses only fish-meal as fertilizer, abjuring chemical fertilizers, and prunes the vines severely to limit production. The four stills are big (25 hectolitres) and modern, the ageing exclusively in small oak casks. M. Thomas is emphatic that he never uses any additives.

CHATEAU DE FONTPINOT

See Frapin.

CHATEAU-PAULET

Château-Paulet, Domaine de la Couronne Route de Segonzac, B.P. 24, 16101 Cognac ***Tel: (45) 32 07 00***
Paulet Ecusson Rouge · Paulet VSOP · Paulet Napoléon · Paulet Vieille (FC) XO · Extra Vieille Réserve Louis XVI (FC) · Borderies Très Vieilles · Château Paulet Age Inconnu

Founded in 1848 at the delightful château. By the end of the 19th century Jean-Maurice Lacroux started to sell the firm's cognacs under the name of the château. Today it is run by his descendant, Bernard Lacroux, who now has no vines of his own and only seven small relatively new stills. Cognacs are bought in from the Champagnes, Borderies and Fins Bois only. It has an excellent reputation, and supplies choosy outlets like Harrods.

CHATEAU SAINT-SORLIN

Madame Castelnau-Gros, St-Sorlin de Cognac, 17150 Mirambeau ***Tel: (46) 86 01 27***
XXX (FB) 3+ · Napoléon (FB) 6+ · Hors d'Age (FB) 15+

M. Carrière, the great-grandfather of Madame Castelnau-Gros, was a nurseryman, one of the group of Charentais who went to the USA after the onset of phylloxera, to find rootstocks suitable for use in Cognac. The 20 hectares of vines owned by his great-granddaughter are in the chalky pocket by the Gironde just opposite Château Loudenne. Madame Castelnau-Gros is a real enthusiast, selling her cognacs to 5,000 private clients and 200 groups in factories. She likes her cognac well coloured with caramel and slightly sweetened with syrup.

CHOLLET

Jacques Chollet, Le Planty, Boutiers-Saint-Trijan, 16100 Cognac ***Tel: (45) 32 12 93***
VS 3 · VSOP 5 · Napoléon 8 · XO 13
Marquis de Vallade
M. Chollet began by supplying wine to Salignac from his 18 hectare estate in the best of the Fins Bois. Then built four substantial stills to supply them with cognac. After Salignac was taken over by Courvoisier, its purchases declined, and in 1977 M. Chollet started to sell his own cognacs. Four of M. Chollet's eight children now work with him.

Success means that his own grapes now account for only one-fifth of his requirements. M. Chollet likes his cognacs soft: sells mostly to French private clients, but also exports to the USA under the names both of Chollet and Marquis de Vallade.

CLAIR

P. Clair, Neuillac, 17520 Archiac ***Tel: (46) 48 15 43***
XXX (PC) 6 · VSOP (PC) 15 · Hors d'Age (PC)
Small family estate of 13 hectares on the choicest slopes of the Petites Champagnes d'Archiac. The Clair family has been selling its cognacs to the public since 1935 at which time it built a small (15.5 hectolitre) alembic. It still relies on its own production for 90% of sales, which are mostly VSOP, mainly to private clients and factory groups. It uses traditional methods, and no chemical weedkillers. But M. Clair likes his cognacs smooth and soft, adding up to 2% of *boisé* to his products when he blends them.

PASCAL COMBEAU

See Gemaco.

COMPAGNIE COMMERCIALE DE GUYENNE (CCG)

26, Rue Pascal Combeau, Cognac ***Tel: (45) 82 32 10***
Founded in 1976 by one of the most remarkable men in Cognac, Michel Coste, formerly manager of Otard. He has gradually bought up a number of old-established firms, including Lucien-Foucauld and Meukow, and is a major supplier to French supermarkets.

COMTE DE DAMPIERRE

Château de Plassac, 17240 St-Genis-de-Saintonge
Tel: (46) 49 81 85
VSOP (BB) 7 · Napoléon (BB) 11 · XO (BB) 15
This estate of 30 hectares in the best part of the Bons Bois just west of Jonzac has been a family holding since the château was built in 1769.

GILLES COSSON

La Grange Neuve, Guimps, 16300 Barbezieux
Tel: (45) 78 90 37
VSOP (FC) 7 · VSOP Blason (FC) 10 · Vieille Réserve (FC) 25 · XO (FC)
This old established family sells only cognacs from its 50 hectares of vines in both Champagnes.

COURVOISIER

Place du Château, 16200 Jarnac *Tel: (45) 81 04 11*
XXX up to 7 · VSOP (FC) up to 15 · Napoléon (FC) up to 30 · XO up to 60
Visits in summer 8.30–11.30 a.m. and 2–5 p.m.
Always the odd man out among the Big Four in Cognac, largely because it has never been a truly native firm, has never owned vineyards (or major stocks of brandies), and never played a major role in the social or political life of the region. It was founded by Emmanuel Courvoisier, a native of the Jura, whose main interests were his warehouses in Bercy on the outskirts of Paris. Nevertheless, he established himself as the cognac supplier to the Court of Napoléon I. His son Felix enlarged his father's business, but it was only in 1869, three years after his death (and a year before the Emperor was deposed) that Courvoisier was appointed: "Purveyor by Special Appointment to the Court of Napoléon III".

Felix Courvoisier left his business to two nephews, the Curlier brothers, who lived in Cognac. But in 1909 they sold it to other absentee owners, the Simons, Anglo-French brothers with major wine businesses in both Paris and London. They cleverly exploited the firm's connection with the Napoléon family: the shadow of Napoléon I on its bottles became Cognac's most recognizable trademark at a time when many dubious spirits were being sold as cognac.

Courvoisier was confiscated by the Germans during the Occupation. In the 1950s Christian Braastad, a member of a remarkable Norwegian family (*see also* Delamain), made it one of the most important firms in the industry – vying with Martell for top place in the expanding French market. In the early 1960s it suffered from its historic policy of keeping the minimum possible stocks; in 1964 it was sold to the Canadian drinks group Hiram Walker (itself sold to the British group, Allied-Lyons, in 1986). For a few years in the 1970s Courvoisier was the best-selling brand of cognac, thanks to Hiram Walker's world sales network, but it has now slipped.

The firm's style is unmistakable, richer, smoother, more caramelly than any other – although Courvoisier uses less than 1% of caramel, and that purely to standardize the colour. The blends, too, are interesting. Courvoisier has only 100 stills including those owned by distillers with whom it works) and buys grapes for them only from the Fins Bois – the lowest *cru* used. Both the next qualities are Fine Champagne (the Napoléon contains much more than the legal minimum of 50% Grand Champagne). But the relatively new – and more expensive – XO has more power than the firm's other cognacs, probably because it contains a proportion of cognacs from the Borderies.

CROIZET

B.P.3, 16720 Saint-Même-Les-Carrières
Tel: (45) 81 90 11
XXX · VSOP · Napoléon · XO · Réserve des Héritiers 40+ · 25 Ans · 50 Ans · Millésimes: 1960, 1963, 1966, 1967

Founded in 1805, although the Croizet family had been growing grapes in the Charente since the 17th century. The firm has always been important – Léon Croizet was awarded the Légion d'Honneur for the part he played in helping to replant the vineyard with American grafted vines. In 1892 a Mlle Croizet married a M. Eymard (the Réserve des Héritiers carries the family wedding portrait). The firm is still run by M. Philippe Eymard.

The firm sells a lot of relatively ordinary cognacs, some from as far afield as the Bois Ordinaires. Its pride and joy are its better quality cognacs from the family vineyards, 150 hectares in the Grande Champagne, which feed the five modern stills accounting for three-fifths of the firm's needs. It has a substantial stock of old cognacs, including 4,000 bottles of pre-phylloxera cognacs – not only from the Grande Champagne but also from the favoured corner of the Fins Bois just north of its headquarters. Hence even its finest offerings are an unusual mixture of Grand Champagne and (fine) Fins Bois. It maintains its stock control is strict enough to guarantee the age of its 25- and 50-year-old cognacs.

The French authorities have been so impressed by M. Eymard's book-keeping that he has been allowed to sell some of his cognacs as coming from specific vintages.

CRYSTAL DRY

See Castel Sablons.

DE LAAGE

See Gemaco.

DELAMAIN

Rue J. & R. Delamain, PO Box 16, 16200 Jarnac
Tel: (45) 81 08 24
Pale & Dry (GC) 25 · Vesper (GC) 35 · Très Vieux (GC) 50 · Réserve de la Famille (GC) 55

Both the firm itself and the cognacs it sells are unique. In 1625 Nicolas Delamain, a Jarnaçais, emigrated to England in the suite of Henrietta Maria, sister of the French King Louis XIII and wife of Charles I of England. The family subsequently emigrated to Ireland (where they founded a famous porcelain factory), but in 1759 James Delamain returned to his ancestral home. Three years later he joined his father-in-law, Isaac Ranson, who owned an old firm of cognac merchants.

In the 19th century the Delamains' cousins, the Roullets, entered the business which became Roullet & Delamain. In 1920 it became simply Delamain and remains a family firm, since the mother of the present chairman, Alain Braastad, was a Mlle Delamain. Both sides are distinguished: Alain Braastad's father ran Courvoisier (qv), while in the first half of the century the Delamains achieved distinction as authors

(Robert Delamain wrote the best book on cognac), archaeologists, entomologists and publishers.

Alain Braastad faithfully follows the family tradition, producing cognacs tailored to the historic taste of aristocratic British connoisseurs. The firm only buys brandies at least 15 years old from a few growers, all in the Grande Champagne, keeping them for at least another 10 years in one of the region's most picturesque warehouses. None of its brandies has ever seen any new oak. They are all Pale & Dry, appropriately the name of the brand which accounts for four-fifths of its sales. All Delamain's cognacs have the intensity and elegance of some fine clarets.

DELPECH FOUGERAT

SARL J. Delpech & Fils, Barret, 16300 Barbezieux
Tel: (45) 78 06 01
Delpech-Fougerat:
VS 4 · VSOP 7 · Napoléon 15 · XO 25 · Vielle Réserve (PC)
Saunier de Longchamps:
VS (FB) 3 · VSOP (FB) 5
Logis de La Fontaine:
Grande Champagne

Growers since 1777, Delpech Fougerat claims to be amongst the first to distil cognac in the Barbezieux region. The company is the proud owner of three major properties in the Petite Champagne which supply all the cognacs sold under the family name. The firm maintains a distinctive dry style owing something to the fact that it still has quite a lot of Folle Blanche and Colombard grapes. The brandies for the Saunier brand are bought from a single grower in the Fins Bois.

DENIS-MOUNIE

BP 14, 16200 Jarnac ***Tel: (45) 81 05 38***
XXX 5 · VSOP (FC) 10 · Napoléon · XO · Edouard VII Très Vieille (FC) 25 · Extra Très Vieille (GC) 40

Founded in 1838 by two vineyard owners, Justin Denis and Henri Mounié. Achieved fame and fortune after that great gourmand, King Edward VII, developed a taste for their 1865 Grande Champagne. The firm remained in family hands and its reputation stayed high until it was bought by Bénédictine in 1969. The firm is making something of a comeback since Hine (qv) bought it in 1982.

DOMAINE DES BRISSONS DE LAAGE

SARL Bertrand et Fils, Domaine des Brissons de Laage, Reaux, 17500 Jonzac ***Tel: (46) 48 09 03***
XXX (PC) 5–8 · VSOP (PC) 10–15 · Napoléon (PC) 20 · Vieille Réserve (PC) 25

M. Raymond Bertrand, the owner, comes from a long line of growers, brokers and merchants. All the brandies come from his fine 72 hectare estate, the historic Domaine des Brissons de Laage in the heart of the Petite Champagne. Half is sold privately in France, the other half within Europe. The style is deliberately darker and more intense than is normal, not because of any additives but because the cognacs are kept longer than is usual.

DOMAINE DE FAUCAUDAT

Gilbert Ricard, Juillac Le Coq, 16130 Segonzac
Tel: (45) 83 00 35
VSOP (GC) 6 · Hors d'Age "Age unknown"
M. Ricard has been selling the production from his 11 hectares of vines in the Grande Champagne since 1958.

DOMAINE DE MONTIFAUD

17520 Archiac *Tel: (46) 49 50 77*
XXX (PC) 4 · VSOP (PC) 8 · Napoléon (PC) 15 · Hors d'Age (PC) 30
The family sells only cognacs from its 50 hectares of vines in the famous Petites Champagnes d'Archiac.

DOR

4 Bis Rue Jacques Moreau, 16200 Jarnac
Tel: (45) 81 03 26
Hors d'Age (GC) Réserve · Réserve No. 7 42° · Extra No. 9 1914 · Age d'Or 1893 36° · Excellence 1889 35° · Prince Imperial 1875 36° · Napoléon III Empereur 1858 37° · Louis Philippe 1840 34° · Roi de Rome 1811 31° · The Oldest 1805 31°
The firm still owns some of the pre-phylloxera cognacs originally bought by Amadée-Edouard Dor soon after he founded it in 1858. The cognacs are now in demijohns – their strength ranging from 37° to 30°. The family sells a number of these ancient relics – by a special dispensation it is even allowed to date them. Stocks are replenished from the 20 hectares they own in the Petite Champagne.

L'ENCLOUSE DES VIGNES

Famille Renou-Bourreau, Mageloup, Floirac, 17120 Cozes *Tel: (46) 90 63 29*
XXX 8–10 · Spécial 65° 8–10 · VSOP 15 · Réserve Familiale 25–30
Enterprising family headquartered in a forgotten corner of the Cognac region south of Royan, though their 30 hectares of vines are in the Fins Bois and the Petite Champagne, as well as in the Bons Bois. The firm has been selling its own cognacs since 1935, mostly to private clients within France.

EXSHAW

127 Boulevard Denfert Rochereau, 16100 Cognac
Tel: (45) 82 40 00
No 1 (GC) · Age d'Or (GC) 40–50
Until recently a famous name, especially in Britain, where Exshaw ranked with Hine and Delamain. Founded in 1805, Exshaw was important in Britain and in India (before the Suez canal, camels were used to carry brandy across the Isthmus of Suez). After 1945 the firm dwindled into insignificance. In 1975 it was bought by Otard (qv) which is trying to revive its fortunes by concentrating exclusively on cognacs from the Grande Champagne with plenty of *rancio*.

FALANDY-LIANDRY

6, Rue de Barbezieux, Cognac *Tel: (45) 35 02 25*
Napoléon · VR · XO · Très Vieille Réserve
Family company famous mainly because its Très Vieille

Réserve, at around £300 the bottle, is the most expensive cognac sold in that choosiest of markets, Hong Kong.

FAUCON D'OR

See Gemaco.

PIERRE FERRAND

La Nérolle, 16130 Segonzac ***Tel: (45) 83 41 82***
Réserve de la Proprieté (GC) 12 · Sélection des Anges (GC) 25 · Réserve Ancestrale (GC) 50
"It is the Good Lord himself who slips down the throat in carpet slippers" is how M. Ferrand describes his cognacs. He is more entitled to his lyricism than many rivals. The family has been distilling from its own grapes since 1702 – in buildings enclosed by the typical shuttered Charentais farmyard. Today M. Ferrand sells only brandies made from grapes grown on his 27 hectares in the best of the Grande Champagne, ensuring a rare depth and intensity. He sells two-thirds of his production outside France, much of the best in special bottles as New Year gifts.

JEAN FILLIOUX

Le Pouyade, Juillac-le-Coq, 16130 Segonzac
Tel: (45) 83 04 09
Coq (GC) 3 · Spéciale Amateur (GC) 44° 3 · Napoléon (GC) 7+ · Cep d'Or (GC) 7+ · Spéciale Amateur (GC) 42° 7+ · Très Vieux (GC) 7+
Founded in 1880 by Honoré Fillioux, a rogue member of the family which has blended cognacs for Hennessy (qv) for seven generations. The tradition of selling cognacs from the family property of 16 hectares in the Grande Champagne is now upheld by Honoré's great-grandson Pascal. The firm also sells cognacs from the properties of two other families.

LA FINE GOULE

Le Patis, 17520 Archaic ***Tel: (46) 49 10 14***
Junior (PC) 5 · VSOP (PC) 8 · Napoléon (PC) 12 · Hors d'Age (FC) 25 · Très Vieux (PC) 40
For the past 10 years the Larquier and Magnand families have sold the cognacs from their 41 hectares of vines in the Petites Champagnes d'Archiac. They pride themselves on ageing their cognacs as long as possible and on the (numbered) bottles of old cognac sold at their natural strength of 43.7° (which makes them around 50 years old).

MICHEL FORGERON

Chez Richon, 16130 Segonzac ***Tel: (45) 83 43 05***
XXX (GC) 4 · VSOP (GC) 43° 10 · Vieille Réserve (GC) 45° 15 · Hors d'Age Spéciale (GC) 50°
20 years ago Michel Forgeron and his wife took over the family farm of 11 hectares in the Grande Champagne, installed a still, and concentrated exclusively on the grapes, Pineau de Charentes and cognac. They started to sell their own cognac in 1977. Madame Forgeron says: "the expansion of our sales doubtless suffers from our passion for our vines and for our cognac to which we devote so much of our time". They admit adding up to 0.5% of *boisé* in their younger qualities. But, sensibly, they sell their older cognacs stronger

than is usual, reckoning that the most fiery ethers will have evaporated by the time they are bottled, leaving a cognac with a truly intense bouquet.

FOUGERAT
See Delpech Fougerat.

FRANCOIS DE MARTIGNAC
See Guy de Bersac.

FRAPIN
Rue Pierre Frapin, F-16130 Segonzac
Tel: (45) 83 40 03
XXX · Flamme Royale (GC) 60° · VSOP (GC) · Napoléon (GC) · XO (GC) · Domaine Frapin (GC) · Château de Fontpinot (GC)
One of the most extraordinary stories in Cognac. The firm is the only one based in Segonzac, the heart of the Grande Champagne. Its fame and fortune was founded on the extensive family estates, amounting to 350 hectares in the Grande Champagne. These were inherited by the wife of M. André Renaud who built up Rémy Martin (qv). Eventually they all passed to his younger daughter, Madame Max Cointreau, the minority shareholder in Rémy Martin.

In the mid-1970s, as a result of a bitter and continuing family row, Rémy stopped buying Frapin's cognacs. Since then the Cointreaus have been exploiting their inheritance. Their range starts with a Three-Star which they frankly recommend for cocktails, and a Flamme Royale, a super-strength cognac designed to flambé dishes. Their more serious cognacs all come from their estates. All have spent a relatively long time in new wood and are richer and more intense than most cognacs. At their best – like the Château de Fontpinot, a rare single-domaine cognac, exclusively from the 137 hectares around the château – the cognacs are fruity enough to absorb the tannins from the new wood which gives them considerable, but balanced, power. Irritatingly the Cointreaus will not give the age of their cognacs.

A DE FUSSIGNY
Alain & Anne-Marie Royer, 60 Rue des Moulins, 16200 Jarnac ***Tel: (45) 81 62 59***
Vieille Réserve Series Rares (FC) · XO Lot 099 · Très Vieille Grande Champagne Series Rares
An enterprising new venture owned by Alain Royer, who was responsible for the introduction of some exciting old cognacs when he worked with his family firm, Louis Royer (qv). He is now marketing a series of old cognacs bought from growers in the Grande Champagne, the Petite Champagne d'Archiac and the Fins Bois de Jarnac. His blends are all old-fashioned, with an elegance and an intensity which owe nothing to additives. As individual lots are exhausted he will move to another number, emphasizing that old cognacs should not be forced into a uniform house style.

GAUTIER
29 Rue des Ponts, 16140 Aigre ***Tel: (45) 21 10 02***

XXX · VSOP · Napoleon · XO · Royale · Extra (The higher grades are sold in a number of special decanters, including one shaped like a ship's bell, as well as in a Limoges porcelain flask shaped like Concorde)
In 1644 Charles Gautier married the daughter of a local grower near Aigre, then an important trading centre. The firm was founded a century later and remained in family hands until 1970 when it was bought by the Berger group, best known for its pastis, which also controls Gemaco (qv).

HENRI GEFFARD
Verrières, 16130 Segonzac ***Tel: (45) 83 02 74***
XXX (GC) 6 · VSOP (GC) 10 · Vieille Réserve (GC) 13
M. Geffard maintains a due balance between tradition and modernity, distilling in modern premises among vines on which he refuses to use herbicides. The family has grown vines since 1880, but M. Geffard has sold the cognacs from his two properties in the Grande Champagne (at Verrières and Juillac-le-Coq) for only 10 years.

GEMACO
28 Rue des Ponts, 16140 Aigre ***Tel: (45) 21 10 02***
Pascal Combeau: VSOP · Napoléon · XO
DeLaage Faucon d'Or: XXX · VSOP
Girard: VSOP (FC)
Normandin: XXX · Napoléon · Fine Champagne · Réserve Spéciale (GC)
Holding company, owned by Berger, the pastis group. Berger also owns Gautier (qv). Gemaco includes other old-established family companies bought by Berger, whose brands it uses for specific markets. Its subsidiaries include Pascal Combeau, founded by a local worthy in 1838, whose products, often in special flasks, are sold in duty free outlets: Faucon d'Or, a brand belonging to de Laage, founded in 1856, and taken over by Berger in 1971; E. Normandin, founded in 1844; and Girard, founded in 1884.

GIRARD
See Gemaco.

PAUL GIRAUD
Bouteville, 16120 Châteauneuf sur Charente
Tel: (45) 97 03 93
VSOP (GC) 6 · Napoléon (GC) 12 · Vieille Réserve (GC) 20
The Girauds have grown grapes at Bouteville, in the heart of the Grande Champagne, since 1650, but have sold the product of their 28 hectares of vines, and their two – modern – stills for the last 10 years only.

The firm is lucky in having extremely moist cellars, which give its prize-winning cognacs a softness not found in some other Grande Champagnes. It is much attached to the ideas of purity and tradition and so uses as little insecticide as possible. Although Giraud uses up to 0.75% of sugar it eschews any caramelization, and indeed, is proud of selling its relatively light coloured cognacs.

GODET
1 Rue du Duc, 17000 La Rochelle ***Tel: (46) 41 10 66***
XXX 2 · Gastronome (FC) 7–8 · Napoléon 15 · EX (FC) 10 · XO (FC) 20
The Godets are an integral part of the history of Cognac. They are descended from a Dutch family which settled in La Rochelle around 1600, when the Dutch were teaching the French how to distil *brandywijn.*

The family started by exporting cognac in cask and has been established as a firm since 1838 in La Rochelle, at the very edge of the Cognac region. Godet remains a traditional merchant, selling in Europe and the Far East as well as in France. It has no vines or stills of its own, buying its cognacs young from growers in the Fins Bois, the Bois Ordinaires and the Champagnes.

LEOPOLD GOURMEL
BP 194, 16016 Cognac ***Tel: (45) 82 07 29***
Age du Fruit 8 · Age des Fleurs 10 · Age des Epices 13 · Quintessence 20
A delightful story, resulting in a fine and unusual range of cognacs. Pierre Voisin, the owner, worked for a long time in the car industry, first as a quality controller at Fiat, then as a Volvo dealer.

M. Voisin, however, loved cognacs, especially the light, under appreciated cognacs from the Fins Bois. The storage, blending and tasting of these cognacs became a hobby. At the urging of his wife and daughter Caroline he gradually transformed his obsession into his livelihood.

M. Voisin owns no vines, distils none of his own cognacs, but relies on three growers only. The two biggest are in the Grande Champagne and the best corner of the Fins Bois de Jarnac. M. Voisin also buys a little wine from the Petite Champagne which is distilled for him. He ensures that the wines are distilled on their lees and the spirit to a low figure – 69°. Both steps are designed to maximize their fruitiness. The cognacs are kept in new wood for only a few months and then transferred and kept exclusively in small casks in damp cellars.

M. Voisin takes unusual care when reducing his cognacs to 40°. He allows 14 months to bring even the cheapest quality down, and between four and five years to reduce his Quintessence. M. Voisin always insists that his brandies epitomize the best of the Fins Bois, so it is something of a shock to see how much Grande Champagne he uses. Nevertheless, all his three better offerings have an unusual delicacy: the Age des Fleurs is appropriately fresh and floral; the Age des Epices is decidedly reminiscent of dried herbs or grass (not as spicy as the name implies); these qualities are even more intense in the Quintessence.

JEAN-MARIE GRENON
17610 Dompierre sur Charente ***Tel: (46) 91 03 74***
Fine 4 · Vieille Fine 7 · Très Vieille Fine 20
Classic small grower with 32 hectares divided between the Petite Champagne and the Borderies. He sells half his production to groups and private clients in France, the other half to West Germany.

GUILLON-PAINTURAUD
Biard, 16130 Segonzac ***Tel: (45) 83 41 95***
VSOP (GC) 5 · Réserve (GC) 10 · Vieille Réserve (GC) 20
Jean Pierre Guillon can trace his family's roots in Biard, the heart of Grande Champagne, back to 1615. He now sells only cognacs from 17 hectares of vines, distilled in his own two stills (one dating back to before World War I). He adds sugar syrup but no caramel and prides himself on the elegance of his cognacs and his stocks – 15 times current sales.

GUY DE BERSAC
Le Chillot de St Preuil, 16130 Segonzac
Tel: (45) 81 95 87
Owned by: Tradition Brillat-Savarin, 60 Avenue de la Bourdonnais, Paris 75007 ***Tel: (1 45) 56 12 20***
Guy de Bersac:
Fine 5 · VSOP 8 · Napoléon 12 · Grande Fine Champagne 15–20 · Très Vieille Fine 30
Trois Empereurs:
VSOP 8 · XO Spécial 15–20
François du Martignac
Subsidiary of an important French drinks marketing group, selling over two million bottles of cognac a year, largely abroad. No vines or stills of its own, buys in Petite Champagne, Borderies, Fins Bois and Bons Bois.

PIERRE HARD
Allée des Tilleuls, Château de Brizambourg, 17770 Brizambourg
VSOP 10 · Napoléon 15 · Vieille Réserve 20
A small property in the Fins Bois, selling the output of 15 hectares of vines both in France and Germany – clearly believes in ageing its cognacs.

A. HARDY
BP 27, 147 Rue Basse, de Croun, 16100 Cognac
Tel: (45) 82 59 55
Red Corner XXX 3 · VSOP 5+ · Noces d'Or (FC) 50
The Hardys, probably of English descent, started as local distillers. Antoine Hardy was a broker on behalf of English buyers who founded his own firm in 1863. He specialized in selling to Russia, shutting his London office when sales slumped after a duty increase. His son Valéri developed Anglophobia and the firm's natural concentration on the Russian and Central European markets served it badly. One of Valéri's six grandsons, Francis, was the long-serving Deputy and Mayor of Cognac. Although the firm is now partly owned by the Crédit Commercial de France, it is still run by the Hardy family.

JAS HENNESSY
1, Rue de la Richonne, 16101 Cognac
Tel: (45) 82 52 22
VS 3–10 · VSOP Fine Champagne 5–25 · Napoléon 8–30 · XO 10–70 · Paradis 15–100
Visits to cellars and cooperage museum from 1 June to 15 September every day (except Sundays and bank holidays)

from 8.30 a.m.–5.30 p.m. Rest of the year from 8.30–11 a.m. and 1.45–4.30 p.m. (except weekends and bank holidays).

Hennessy is now, by any measure, the biggest firm in Cognac, selling well over 20 million bottles a year. This is not new. With Martell, its friendly rival, it has been one of the leaders in the trade ever since it was founded in 1765 by Richard Hennessy, descendant of Irish Catholic immigrants, and an officer in the French army. He flourished as "Citizen Hennessy" in the French Revolution. The Hennessys remained important as Liberal politicians devoted to Free Trade throughout the 19th century, but gradually became more aristocratic. This had its advantages – Hennessy not only had a traditional hold on the Irish market but also became popular with the British aristocracy. This however led to a neglect of the French market. Aristocratic carelessness prevented the family from monopolizing its best ideas: Auguste Hennessy invented the award of stars to indicate the age of cognacs; a later Hennessy thought up XO; both ideas are now in general use.

At the turn of the century James Hennessy, disheartened by his wife's death, moved to Paris. In 1922 his son Maurice, already a friend of the Firino-Martell family, engineered a 25-year pact between them. Each took shareholdings in the other's firms and, effectively, divided the world between them. Martell's influence was predominant in Britain, Hennessy in Ireland, the USA and the Far East.

During the German Occupation, Maurice Hennessy was largely responsible for the partnership between merchant and grower which resulted in the Bureau National Interprofessionel du Cognac. The partnership with Martell was dissolved in 1947. But Hennessy has retained its dominant position in some of the markets it was allocated, most notably the United States. It is now Cognac's most important exporter, selling 96% of its production abroad. Sales were helped by the 1971 merger with Moët & Chandon, the aristocratic drinks company. Hennessy, however, is still largely autonomous, and still run by descendants of the founder. The new group, Moët-Hennessy, was big enough to take over their US distributors, Schieffelin, which had been selling Hennessy since the late 18th century. Schieffelin sold nearly 800,000 cases of cognac in the USA in 1985, the largest quantity ever sold in a single market by a single merchant in any one year.

As aspiring aristocrats the Hennessys naturally accumulated much land during the 19th century, and now own 450 hectares of vines. However, these account for less than 5% of the firm's needs. Similarly the firm's 28 distilleries supply far less spirit than the hundreds of stills used by the 2,500 or so growers from whom Hennessy buys wine for distillation and another 700 from whom it buys young brandies.

Hennessy has the most impressive stocks of any Cognac firm: 180,000 casks, equivalent to 87 million bottles. Hennessy's distinctive style owes much to these stocks and the personal taste of the Fillioux family which has blended cognacs (for Hennessy) for seven generations. The Fillioux like their cognacs round, full and fruity. They are also prepared to use plenty of Borderies for this purpose, even in their better blends (although recently they changed the VSOP to Fine Champagne to provide a greater elegance). The Fillioux style is seen at its best in the XO.

HINE

16, Quai de l'Orangerie, 16200 Jarnac
Tel: (45) 81 11 38
Signature · VSOP (FC) · Antique (FC) · Napoléon · XO · Old Vintage (GC) · Triomphe (GC) · Family Réserve (GC)

Hine is one of the most venerable names in Cognac. It was founded by an immigrant from Dorset, Thomas Hine, who settled in Cognac in 1782, married into the Delamain family and became a partner. The firm became well known for the cognacs it shipped in cask to British wine merchants for bottling under its name for sale to the aristocracy (the firm still supplies the British Royal Family). With reluctance Hine accepted the necessity for its own trademark, the stag (this may be a pun, since a hind is a female deer), and only introduced a three star quality after World War II. In 1971 Hine was bought by the Distillers Company (itself taken over by Guinness in 1986). The firm is still largely run by the cousins Jacques and Bernard Hine, the founder's great-great-great grandsons.

Bernard Hine, a well-known taster, still blends Hine's cognacs to maintain the family's tradition for elegance and lightness. Hine has neither vines nor stills of its own, buying half its cognacs young, the other old. Hine uses only small casks of Limousin oak. The Hine style excludes the Borderies, so the cognacs are exclusively from the Champagnes and the Premiers Fins Bois.

JULLIARD

SARL Cognac-Pineau Julliard, Perignac, 17800 Pons ***Tel: (46) 96 30 42/41 04***
VSOP (PC) 6 · Réserve (PC) 15

A small grower selling only his own cognacs from an estate in a village in the heart of Petite Champagne by the side of a magnificent 12th century Romanesque church. Honestly admits to using *boisé* and caramel to improve his cognacs.

JULLIEN

A. Jullien, Logis de la Mothe, Criteuil, 16300 Barbezieux ***Tel: (45) 80 54 02***
Grand Champagne 12

The Jullien family has owned 61 hectares in the Grande Champagne since 1865.

LAFITE

Société Civile du Château Lafite Rothschild, 17 Avenue Matignon, 75008 Paris ***Tel: (1 42) 56 32 50***
Très vieille Réserve

The first product to emerge from the stable of spirits being launched by Baron Eric de Rothschild, controlling partner of the company which runs the Rothschild family's vineyards. The result is worthy of the name: a rich, dense, woody blend of old cognacs, up to 80 years old, some from the Borderies, but also from the Champagnes.

GASTON DE LAGRANGE

7, Rue de la Pierre Levée, Châteaubernard, 16100 Cognac ***Tel: (45) 82 18 17***

XXX 4–5 · VSOP (FC) 8–15 · Napoleon 8–15 · XO (GC) 40+

Visits from Monday to Friday, 9 a.m.–12 noon and 2–6 p.m.

No, there is no M. Lagrange. The firm was founded in 1961 by Martini & Rossi, the Italian group. It has 15 hectares of vines in the Borderies, but no stills of its own. Buys brandies only in the four best regions.

REMI LANDIER

Domaine du Carrefour (GAEC), Cors de Foussignac, 16200 Jarnac ***Tel: (45) 81 14 52***

XXX (FB) 4 · VSOP (FB) 8 · Vieille Réserve (FB) 15 · Très Vieux Napoléon (FB) 20

Substantial third-generation family business in the heart of Premiers Fins Bois de Jarnac. Naturally, but unusually, his labels proclaim that all his cognacs are from the Fins Bois.

LANDRY

Jacques Landry, Logis de Beaulieu, 17520 Germignac ***Tel: (46) 49 13 67***

Cognac de Propriétaire (FC) 18

Since 1972 M. Landry has been selling cognac from his 19 hectares in the much-valued Petites Champagnes d'Archiac, on the banks of the River Né opposite the Grande Champagne. M. Landry is fortunate to own a house dating back to the end of the 16th century, with a superb pigeon loft. His six stills are a mixture of ancient and modern, one dating back 100 years. M. Landry, whose main business is buying and selling Esprit de Cognac, adds 3% *boisé* to his cognac six months after it has been distilled.

LARSEN

66, Boulevard de Paris, BP41, 16100 Cognac ***Tel: (45) 82 05 88***

Spécial · VSOP Viking · TVFC · Napoléon · Golden Viking Hors d'Age · Extra (Also FC cognacs in bottles shaped like Viking ships and a horse made of Limoges porcelain)

Old-established family business. It used to sell in cask mainly to the state monopolies of its native Scandinavia. The firm still buys in all its cognacs (exclusively from growers in the Fins Bois and the Champagnes). Sales in Scandinavia now account for less than one-fifth of the total as Larsen now concentrates on selling better grade cognac, often in fancy containers, in the Far East. Larsen prides itself on lightness, but strength of character, of its cognacs.

LHERAUD

Domaine de Lasdoux, Angeac Charente, 16120 Châteauneuf ***Tel: (45) 97 12 33***

XXX Spécial (FC) 8 · VSOP (FC) 12 · Réserve du Templier (FC) 10 · Vieille Réserve du Templier (FC) 42° 25 · Très Vieille Réserve du Paradis 52° 50 (FC)

One of the best growers, selling only its own cognacs. The

Lhéraud family have lived at Lasdoux since 1639 and now own 62 hectares on some of the best slopes in the Petite Champagne. It has distilled wines for more than a century but has sold under its own name only since 1971. M. Lhéraud spends much of his time selling his cognacs at France's innumerable country fairs, but is now as well-known in Britain as in France. M. Lhéraud has 10% each of Colombard and Folle Blanche, which help to enrich his blends. Although he uses new oak the cognacs remain elegant and balanced, partly because he does not add any *boisé*, syrup or caramel. The VSOP, in particular, is one of the best on the market, albeit still young and a bit fiery.

LOGIS DE LA FONTAINE

See Delpech Fougerat.

LOGIS DE LA MONTAGNE

Bonnin et Cie, "Logis de la Montagne", Challignac, 16300 Barbezieux ***Tel: (45) 78 52 71***

Logis de la Montagne XXX (FB) 4 · Logis de la Montagne VSOP (FC) 8 · Logis de la Montagne Vieille Réserve (FB) 12 · Vicomte Stephane de Castelbajac Réserve (FB) 12 · VSOP Vicomte Stephane de Castelbajac (FB) 8

M. Bonnin is best known for his prize-winning Pineaus de Charente. He sells much of his cognac in Britain, Holland and West Germany. The Bonnins have been growers for four generations and now own 30 hectares in the far southeast of the Fins Bois – a very chalky area much favoured by buyers for the big firms who like the delicacy of its brandies. Indeed, M. Bonnin still sells some of his production to one of them and uses *boisé* when the cognacs are young.

LOGIS DE MONTIFAUD

Pierre Landreau, Montifaud, Salles d'Angles, 16130 Segonzac ***Tel: (45) 83 71 26***

XXX (FC) 10 · Réserve (GC) 20 · Vieux Cognac (GC) 50

M. Landreau sells only cognacs from his 17 hectares of vines, mostly in the Grande Champagne. He keeps his cognacs a long time, and does not use any additives.

LUCIEN-FOUCAULD

See Compagnie Commerciale de Guyenne.

MARAY-JOLY

See Roussile.

MARCHIVE

SARL René & Gilles Marchive, Logis de Scée, Vars, 16630 St Amant de Boixe ***Tel: (45) 21 44 34***

XXX (FB) 3 · VSOP (FB) 5 · Napoléon (FB) 15 · Très Vieille Réserve (FB) 40

The Marchive family has grown grapes for four generations, living in its 11th century farmhouse in the far northeast of the Fins Bois since 1872. It now sells cognacs exclusively from its 26 hectares of vines, distilled in two modern stills.

MARQUIS DE ST MAIGRIN
GAF Le Château de St Maigrin, St Maigrin, 17520 Archiac *Tel: (45) 78 47 40*
VSOP (BB) 55 · Vieille Réserve (BB) 6–10 · Grande Réserve Extra (BB)
The Château de St Maigrin on the label is imposing, if rather vulgar. The estate is less impressive: a mere 23 hectares in the unfashionable Bons Bois, albeit in far the best part, just south of Barbezieux. The present owners are related to M. Dettling, who makes the best kirsch in the world, so are likely to be conscious of the need for quality.

MARQUIS DE SAUVAL
See Prunier.

MARQUIS DE VALLADE
See Chollet.

MARTELL
Place Edouard Martell, 16101 Cognac
Tel: (45) 82 44 44
XXX (VS) 5-7 · Médaillon (VSOP) 10–12 · Cordon Rubis 12–18 · Cordon Noir Napoléon 15–20 · Cordon Bleu 20–30 · Cordon Argent/Extra 50+
Visits from Monday to Friday, 8.30–11 a.m. and 2–5 p.m. Open as well on Saturdays in July and August.
The oldest of Cognac's major firms, the least inclined to talk about itself, and thus the easiest to underestimate. In 1715 Jean Martell arrived in Cognac from his native Jersey, then a centre for smuggling brandy into Britain, probably to secure supplies. He married the daughters of two Cognac merchants. The second, Rachel Lallemand, was descended from one of the earliest brandy merchants in Cognac. After Jean's death she carried on under the name of Veuve Martell-Lallemand. Martell became the leading firm in Cognac during the revolutionary period, and is still one of the two largest.

In the mid-19th century control passed to the Firino-Martell, who had married into the Martell family and continue to control the business (although it is a quoted company). The firm reasserted its dominance after the phylloxera. The Firino-Martell built magnificent new distileries, indeed its sprawl of cellars and warehouses in the heart of Cognac, with 16 bottling lines, is almost a town within a town.

Martell flourished by hard, painstaking selling of its brandies to pubs and cafés in France and Britain – both markets where it is still the leader. The half-bottle of "medicinal brandy" found in even the humblest British home was almost invariably from Martell. The firm inevitably ossified during the years 1922–47 when the Firino-Martell went into partnership with Hennessy (qv). Since the dissolution of the relationship its dominance in both traditional markets has been further eroded.

In the 19th century both the firm and the family built up considerable landholdings. The firm now owns 42 hectares in the Grande Champagne, 133 in the Petite Champagne and 90 in the Borderies, while the family owns 53 hectares in the Grande Champagne, 44 in the Petite, 8 in the Boderies and 20 in the Fins Bois. Even so these account for a mere 5% of the firm's needs. Its 28 stills are fed from the estates and by wine from 2,600 growers in the four major *crus*. Martell also buys over half of its requirements, not as wines, but as young brandy from growers in the four top regions.

Martell has its own very particular style of cognac, jealously maintained by the Chapeau family who have blended the firm's cognacs for seven generations (the mother of Pierre Frugier, the present head blender, was a Mlle Chapeau). The style is based on a strong distillation of the cognacs, which provides a relatively neutral base. They are stored mainly in close-grained Tronçais oak, which allows them to mature slowly. The style is admirably suited to the cognacs from the Borderies, which Martell prefers. Indeed, all of their cognacs have a certain nuttiness which comes from blending with the Borderies cognacs. In line with the classic tradition, they are such firm believers in blending that none of their cognacs (not even the excellent Cordon Bleu which for long set the standard for a superior offering from a major firm) are made purely with cognacs from the Champagnes.

MENARD

J. P. Ménard et Fils, 16720 St-Même-les-Carrières
Tel: (45) 81 90 26
Sélection des Domaines (GC) 3–5 · VSOP (GC) 8–10 · Napoléon (GC) 20–25 · Vieille Réserve Extra (GC) 42° 35 · Ancestrale (GC) 50+/-
Family property of 80 hectares where the Ménards have been producing brandy since 1815 and selling it directly – now in West Germany, Belgium and Holland as well as in France – since 1946. Emphasizes authenticity (e.g. in selling its older cognac at its natural strength) and lack of additives.

MENUET

SCA Latonnelle Cognac-Pineau Menuet, 16720 St-Même-Les-Carrières ***Tel: (45) 81 91 55***
XXX (GC) 4 · VSOP (GC) 6 · Vieille Réserve (GC) 12 · Extra (GC) 18 · Vieux Cognac (GC) 40
The Menuets have been making cognacs since 1850, and selling them at least since 1900 when they won a gold medal at the Paris World Exhibition. They now own 50 hectares, all in the Grande Champagne, sell one-tenth of the output of their (modern) still in West Germany, most of the rest to private French customers.

MEUKOW

See Compagnie Commerciale de Guyenne.

MONNET

52 Avenue Paul Firino, 16100 Cognac
Tel: (45) 35 13 40
Le Club 2–5 · VSOP 8–12 · Napoléon 15–20 · XO 25–30 · Josephine 40–45
The firm was founded by the father of Jean Monnet, the statesman known as the "Father of Europe", and arguably Cognac's most famous son. Like Jean-Antoine Salignac

(qv), Monnet's father acted as manager for a group of growers, eventually converting the firm from a cooperative into his own business. He – and his taste for older, finer cognacs – remained famous until World War II. In the 1960s the firm was bought by the German drinks firm Scharlachberg (qv) and now makes a full range of cognacs from the four best growths. It has neither vines nor stills of its own.

MONTAUZIER

Bors-de-Montmoreau, 16190 Montmoreau St Cybard ***Tel: (45) 60 32 86***
Napoléon (BB) 20

One of the few growers in the Bons Bois who markets a superior product. Pierre Montauzier is lucky: his 5 hectares of vines are on the Coteaux de Baffoux, in a corner of the Bons Bois, in the southeast, favoured by some buyers from big firms. He sells only one – additive-free – cognac, aged for 20 years, in specially gold-engraved bottles.

PIERRE MORANDIERE

Le Breuil, Saint George des Agouts, 17150 Mirambeau ***Tel: (46) 86 02 76/49 68 08***
XXX (FB) 4–6 · VSOP (FB) 6–12

An enterprising grower in the far southwest of the Cognac region, in the little patch of chalky soil running back from the Gironde estuary. When M. Morandière inherited some of his father's vines he had the wine distilled by a friend and sold the cognac. He then built suitable premises to store and bottle his production. His sons are extending his range.

MOYET

Etablissements Moyet, 62 Rue de L'Industrie, BP106, 16104 Cognac ***Tel: (45) 82 04 53*** **48 Rue du Château d'Eau, 75010 Paris** ***Tel: (1 42) 08 44 65***

A journalist once described Moyet as "the Antiquaries of Cognac" and the owners, MM. Marc Georges and Pierre Dubarry, promptly took the hint. They admit they stumbled accidentally, but profitably, on the best way to interest the gastronomic world in fine cognac – by offering connoisseurs limited quantities from specific casks of old cognacs.

Moyet itself was a classic small firm, founded in 1864, which achieved its greatest fame at the turn of the century, at which point the family laid down a large stock of fine cognacs. For generations these were largely undisturbed, as the family ceased to take an active interest. The firm was managed by an old *maitre de chai* uninterested in actually selling his precious stocks. When he died, the family decided to sell and M. Georges, a businessman whose wife was a Moyet cousin bought the firm in the late 1970s.

In 1984 a couple of well-known sommeliers tasted some of their older cognacs and suggested that the new owners exploit their inheritance, which they did. Some of their offerings are blends, some come from a single cask, some are undiluted, all are individual and numbered as such. Moyet soon became the smartest of cognacs on the fashion-conscious Parisian scene. To renew their stocks they are now working with the largest *bouilleur de profession* in the region,

Les Viticulteurs Reunis, who have access to stocks held by individual growers as well as its own large stock of old cognacs.

The Moyet Cognacs are all fat, rich, round and young for their age. Tasting a range emphasizes how much is lost by the modern practice of artificially speeding up maturation. Some, of course, lack distinctive character, but at their best have unique overtones of molasses, as well as the strong glow of vanilla, characteristic of the best old-style cognacs.

MUMM

Joseph E Seagram, 375 Park Avenue, New York, NY 10152 ***Tel: (212) 572 7000***
Mumm VSOP 6+
A blend sold only in the USA and named after the champagne (also owned by Seagram). The cognac is left for a further year in oak after being reduced in strength.

NORMANDIN

See Gemaco.

NORMANDIN-MERCIER

Château de la Peraudière, 17139 Dompierre
Tel: (46) 34 28 11
Vieille Fine Champagne 15 · Réserve (GC) 30 · Très Vieille (GC) – before 1914, not reduced · Petite Champagne Vieille 1965 54° · Grande Champagne Vieille 1963 49°
Founded in 1872 by the present owner's great-grandfather, M. Jules Normandin, a broker in Cognac who worked with his mother-in-law, Madame Mercier. Nine years later he bought the Château de la Peraudière, but the family has owned neither vines nor stills. For 25 years after World War II, it specialized in selling old cognacs to the major houses. The firm, then started selling its own blends, often at their original strength, mainly to fine wine specialists in the USA, West Germany and Australia.

OTARD

Château de Cognac, 127 Boulevard Denfert-Rochereau, 16101 Cognac ***Tel: (45) 82 40 00***
VS/XXX · Baron Otard VSOP (FC) 8 · Napoléon · Princes de Cognac (FC) 15
Visits to the Château daily from 9 a.m.–5 p.m.
One of Cognac's most famous names, partly thanks to its ownership of the 16th century Château de Cognac, deservedly the town's most famous historic monument. Founded in 1799 by Jean Dupuy, a local grower, and Jean-Antoine Otard de la Grange, a local landowner who had to be rescued by his tenants from the Revolutionary Terror. He was the descendant of a leading Scottish family devoted to the failing fortunes of the House of Stuart, whom they followed into exile in France. Otard and Dupuy flourished sufficiently to buy the château and become one of Cognac's Big Three in the early 19th century (M. Otard's town house is now Cognac's town hall).

In the early 20th century the family "became more interested in public and social life than in business", according to M. de Ramefort, whose family bought the firm in 1930. His predecessors had relied too heavily on the Latin American market, and "when their competitors began to sell their brandies in bottles under their own names, they declared 'we are not grocers'".

The firm was bought in late 1986 by Bass, the British brewing company, after a period in which the de Rameforts shared control with St Raphael (the aperitif company controlled by Martini.

The firm has never owned any vineyards or stills, however its Baron Otard brand helped re-establish its reputation in the 1970s.

JEAN-LUC PASQUET

Chez Ferchaud, Eraville, 16120 Châteauneuf
Tel: (45) 97 07 49
XXX (PC) 3–4 · Extra (GC) 8 · Napoléon (GC) 15 · Vieille Réserve (GC) 25 · Très Vieux (GC) 50+
Small family grower in the heart of the Grande Champagne. Cognac has been distilled on the site since 1873. He now markets a proportion of the production of his tiny (five hectolitres), 65-year-old still directly, over half of it in West Germany.

ANDRE PETIT

16480 Berneuil ***Tel: (45) 18 55 44***
XXX 4–5 · VSOP 10–12 · Napoléon 20–25 · Vieille Réserve 35–40
Before 1930, M. Jacques Petit used to sell the production of his small (10 hectolitres), 19th century still, with its characteristic onion-shaped *chapiteau*, to Hennessy. M. Petit now has a bigger still as well, but also buys in cognacs from other small producers to reinforce the production of his 15 hectares of vines (one-fifth of them Colombard) in the unfashionable western part of the Fins Bois.

PHILIPPE DE CASTAIGNE

Domaine de Lafont, 16200 Jarnac
Tel: (45) 81 77 36/35 81 72
Philippe de Castaigne:
XXX 5 · Réserve Spéciale VSOP (68cl) 10 (also sold as Very Special Fine Pale) · Napoléon · Réserve Ancienne 25 · Extra Vieux (GC) 35 · Très Vieux: 1893, 1850
Favraud, Château de Souillac:
XXX La Marque du Château · Napoléon · Vieille Réserve la Marque du Château
Of Italian origin, the Castaignes settled in Cognac at the beginning of the 16th century. A century later Gabriel de Castaigne, a descendant and noted alchemist, was almoner to King Henry IV.

The brand was founded in 1860 but had fallen into disuse until in 1980 the name, the fine 17th century château in the heart of the Fins Bois de Jarnac, and its 45 hectares of vines, were acquired by M. and Madame Philippe Vallantin-Dulac. Five years later they bought the old firm of Favraud to help sell their cognacs abroad in the USA and the Far East.

The Domaine has five sizeable modern stills of its own, but M. Vallantin-Dulac also buys cognacs, albeit only from the Champagnes and the Fins Bois de Jarnac. M. Vallantin-Dulac is particularly proud of a novelty item, a "cigar-drink", which, as the name implies, consists of a cigar-shaped glass filled with old cognac.

JEAN PHILIPPON

Jean & Dominique Philippon, "Le Logis de Mosnac", 16120 Châteauneuf ***Tel: (45) 62 53 79***
Napoléon "Tastes 10 years old" · XO "Tastes 15 years old" · Très Vieille Réserve "Tastes 30 years old" · Héritage de mes Aieux 44° 1914
Since 1867, the family has produced cognacs on its 36 hectares of vines on the relatively flat eastern edge of the Petite Champagne on the banks of the Charente. Unusually, Philippon's labels do not advertise the fact that all its cognacs come from the Petite Champagne. Most remarkable is a 1914 vintage cognac, sold at its natural 44°, which, says M. Philippon, "can only be drunk with emotion".

JEAN-CLAUDE PLUCHON

5, Rue Arago, Sillac, 16000 Angoulême
Tel: (45) 91 92 62
Constellation (GC) 8 · Sélection (GC) 12 · Sélection de Luxe (GC) 15
M. Pluchon lives in Angoulême, but owns 10 hectares at Treillis, near Salles D'Angles, in the heart of the Grande Champagne. He does not distil his own cognacs, but stores them in Second Empire premises behind a dignified early 19th century gateway. No additives.

PRINCE HUBERT DE POLIGNAC

49, Rue Lohmeyer, 16102 Cognac ***Tel: (45) 82 45 77***
VS 5–8 · VSOP (FC) 12–15 · Napoléon 18–20 · XO 20+
Paul Bocuse (FC)
Visits every day from 1 July to 15 September from 9 a.m.–1 p.m. and 2–7 p.m. At other times of the year groups only.
The only major cooperative in the Cognac region. All previous efforts have failed, the cooperatives being turned into private firms by their general managers. The 3,500 growers who belong to Unicoop (qv), however, have managed to maintain their independence. The members, who distil 500,000 hectolitres between them, are well scattered: 50% are in the Fins Bois, 33% in the Bons Bois, but only 6% in the Grande Champagne, 9% in the Petite Champagne and 3% in the Borderies. (More variety is provided by the 10% of Colombard grapes).

In 1947 the ancient Polignac family allowed Unicoop to use their name on their own brand of cognacs, since when it has become increasingly important in France (particularly in supermarkets) and 85 foreign countries. The Unicoop eschews additives, but with cognacs from so many sources, over four-fifths in the Bois, it is difficult to establish a very distinct house style – although this does not seem to worry the great chef Paul Bocuse, who buys his cognacs from the cooperative.

PRUNIER

Maison Prunier, 16102 Cognac ***Tel: (45) 82 01 36***
VS · VSOP · Fine Champagne · Napoléon · Family Réserve
Marquis de Sauval: XXX · VSOP · Napoléon

The Prunier family has been shipping cognac since 1700. In 1918 the widow of Alphonse Prunier called in her nephew, Jean Burnez, to help. His son Claude now runs what remains a family-owned business.

MADAME RAYMOND RAGNAUD

Le Château Ambleville, 16300 Barbezieux
Tel: (45) 83 54 57
Haute Roche Réserve (FC) 4+ · Le Château Ambleville Vieille Réserve (GC) 41° 5+ · Le Château Ambleville Réserve Extra (GC) 42° 5+ · Le Château Ambleville Hors d'Age (GC) 43°

Madame Ragnaud is the essence, the ideal of what a direct seller ought to be. She owns only 18 hectares, but these are on the finest slopes in the heart of the Grand Champagne. The ages she attributes are unfair to her cognacs. These have a mellowness which very few Grande Champagnes acquire in less than 10 or 12 years. Even the staunchest believer in blending cannot fail to be moved by the depth, fruitiness and sheer enjoyableness of Madame's offerings.

RAGNAUD SABOURIN

Domaine de la Voute, Ambléville, 16300 Barbezieux ***Tel: (45) 80 54 61***
GC (GC) 4 · VSOP (GC) 10 · Réserve Spéciale (GC) 20 · Fontvieille (GC) 43° 35 · Folle Blanche (GC) 15 · Héritage Ragnaud (GC) "Beginning of the century" · Le Paradis "Beginning of the century" + 10% pre-phylloxera"

About 40 years ago Gaston Briand, then President of the Cognac Growers' Association, started to sell his own cognacs. The business was carried on by his daughter and son-in-law, Denise and Marcel Ragnaud, and is now run by their daughter and son-in-law, Annie and Paul Sabourin.

Deservedly one of the most famous direct sellers, with a major family estate of 50 hectares in the heart of the Grande Champagne, and, unusually, selling twice as much abroad as in France. The classic deep, woody, old-fashioned style is shown to its best in the older cognacs from the family's 15-year stock.

REMY MARTIN

E. Rémy Martin, 20, Rue de la Société Vinicole, BP37, 16102 Cognac ***Tel: (45) 35 16 16***
VS (FC) 3 · VSOP (FC) 7 · Centaure Napoléon (FC) 15–17 · Centaure XO (FC) 22–25 · Centaure Extra (FC) 27–30 · Louis XIII (GC) 50 + (sold in a crystal Baccarat flask modelled on one found at the site of the 16th century Battle of Jarnac)

The most extraordinary success story in modern Cognac. The firm was founded in 1724, but was virtually dormant when it was taken over 200 years later by André Renaud, a grower himself, who had married Mlle Frapin, whose family (qv) owned large estates in the Champagnes. With the help of her family's stocks, and Otto Quien, a Dutch-born sales genius, he developed sales in the Far East, offering only cognacs made in the Champagnes.

After 1945 the firm concentrated on its VSOP, with its frosted glass bottle and map of the region showing the Champagnes, rightly, at the heart. This steadily became the accepted smart cognac in most of the world, especially after Renaud's son-in-law, André Hériard-Dubreuil, took over after his death in 1965. He successfully extended the range up-market with his Centaure cognacs, but was forced to introduce a cheap VS style in Britain and the USA. Today Rémy Martin is, in terms of revenue, one of the top two or three Cognac firms. Like Hennessy, but unlike Courvoisier and Martell, virtually all its sales are outside France.

Rémy Martin remains a family business, albeit bitterly divided. For a decade or more, the family of Madame Max Cointreau, André Renaud's younger daughter, has been fighting the Hériard-Dubreuils in the French courts over a variety of issues connected with their rights as minority shareholders (and as owners of Frapin).

Simultaneously, Hériard-Dubreuil has expanded the business outside Cognac, buying two firms in Champagne, Krug in 1973 and Charles Heidsieck in 1986, the fine wine firm of Nicolas, and the Bordeaux shippers, de Luze. He has even issued shares in the firm which distributes Rémy Martin in the Far East.

Because of its total reliance on cognacs from the Champagnes, which are sold relatively young, the firm has to speed up maturation as much as possible. The wines are distilled on their lees to increase fruitiness, and then kept in – relatively porous – Limousin oak. The resulting style is undeniably smooth and attractive, with some depth and fruit, but without the subtleties found in some other fine cognacs.

RENAULT

Castillon Renault, 23 Rue du Port, 16101 Cognac
Tel: (45) 85 52 88
XXX 3–5 · OVB (Old Vintage Blend) · Carte Noire Extra 10–15 · XO Royal 15–20 · 150ème Anniversaire 50+

Founded in 1835 by Jean Antonin Renault. He was one of the first merchants to export cognac in bottle, thus establishing his brand name. Renault merged with Castillon in 1963, and is now controlled by Louis Dreyfus, the merchants and bankers.

A classic merchant, it buys 30,000 hectolitres of wine from the five best growths to feed its six modern stills, as well as brandies from outside distillers. In the past few years it has abandoned the name Castillon, selling only as Renault. The XXX is sold only in Canada and Ireland, and the OVB only in the Far East.

Over four-fifths of Renault's sales are of the Carte Noire Extra, almost entirely in Scandinavia. Renault use the permitted 2% sugar, and a trace of caramel to standardize the colour, in order to achieve what they describe as a "classic, round, woody style".

JULES ROBIN
36 Rue Gabriel Jaulin, 16100 Cognac
Tel: (45) 82 17 23
XXX · VSOP · Napoléon · XO
Seléction di MM Troisgrois 43° (GC)
Once a famous firm. Founded in 1782 and remained a leader, especially of sales in bottles to Britain, throughout the 19th century. It later concentrated on the Far Eastern markets. The family's alleged collaboration during the war, followed by the loss of its Chinese trade after the Communist takeover in 1949, led to its sale that year to Martell (qv). Now specializes in "soft, mellow" cognacs.

ROLAND RIVIERE
"Saint Pardon", Mortiers, 17500 Jonzac
Tel: (46) 48 61 55
VSOP (FB) 10 · Vieille Réserve (FB) 20 · Vieux Cognac (FB) 40
Family grower with 18 hectares in the favoured southern belt of the Fins Bois. Two-fifths of its sales are to Holland. The firm has sufficient stocks of Grande Champagne to launch a new up-market brand.

ROCHECORAIL
See Roussille.

ROULLET
Le Goulet de Foussignac, 16200 Jarnac
Tel: (45) 81 14 58 **20, Rue Tournefort, 75005 Paris**
Tel: (1) (45) 87 04 00
XXX VS Amber Gold 3+ · VSOP Réserve 6+ · Vieille Réserve/Grande Réserve 11–13 · Extra 20 · Grande Fine (FB) · XO 30 · Très Rare 57 & 60
An attractive mixture of age and enterprise. The Roullet family has grown grapes in the heart of the Premiers Fins Bois de Jarnac for nearly four centuries, at a property centred on a Roman-style house built in the early 17th century. The 22 hectares of vines (which include a little Colombard and Folle Blanche) still supply four-fifths of its requirements.

Roullet is now half-owned by Greene King, the British brewery firm, and is exploiting two of its major assets: the limited stock of very old cognacs kept in glass *jehannes* and sold as Très Rare in limited lots; and the ability to offer an old Fins Bois from the property under the (meaningless) name of Grande Fine. Unusually, most of its sales are abroad. In France it supplies the fine food store of Hédiard.

ROUSSILLE
Linars, 16730 Fleac ***Tel: (45) 91 05 18***
Roussille:
XXX (FB) 4 · VSOP (FB) 8–10 · Vieille Réserve/XO (FB) 20
Domaine de Libourdeau
Maray-Joly
Rochecorail
A property east of the Fins Bois, on the last chalk slopes before Angoulême. The business dates back to 1928 when

Gaston Roussille began to sell his cognac, and is now run by his grandson Christian. Two large modern stills are housed in equally modern buildings. It sells a range of cognacs under different names, one-fifth to West Germany.

ROUYER

Rouyer Guillet, Château de la Roche, 17100 Saintes ***Tel: (46) 93 15 26/01 41***

Brevet Royal 4 · Damoisel VSOP 15 · Rois de France 30 · Philippe Guillet (GC) 80

Established in 1701 by Philippe Guillet. Still run by the same family.

ROI DES ROIS

See Unicognac.

LOUIS ROYER

BP12, 16200 Jarnac ***Tel: (45) 81 02 72***

XXX · VSOP (FC) · Grande Réserve Extra (FC) · Grande Fine Champagne Extra · XO Réserve

Founded in the 19th century, Royer used to specialize in bulk cognacs. A few years ago Alain Royer, the owner's eldest son, started to blend some fine, elegant cognacs, in the style of Delamain and Hine, which he also sold under the name of Jules Duret (an unsuccessful Cognac merchant, painted by Manet, whose firm was subsequently bought by Royer). In 1986 there was a family row, Alain Royer left and founded his own brand, de Fussigny, (qv). Later that year Royer was sold to the Japanese drinks group, Suntory.

ROY RENE

Le Mas, Juillac-le-Coq, 16130 Segonzac
Tel: (45) 83 47 09

A family estate of 30 hectares in the Grande Champagne, making a rich, full, agreeable cognac.

SALIGNAC

Domaine du Breuil, BP No 4, 16101 Cognac
Tel: (45) 81 04 11

XXX 3 · VSOP 6 · Napoléon 7+ · XO

Founded as a cooperative of growers run by Antoine de Salignac, who was joined by his son Pierre-Antoine. In the 1830s they launched a political and commercial challenge to the major merchants. Later Salignac went its own way, selling cognacs in bottle rather than, as the growers preferred, in cask. In 1924 it merged with Henri Roy and is now a subsidiary of Courvoisier.

SAUNIER DE LONGCHAMPS

See Delpech Fougerat.

PIERRE SEGUINOT

"La Nerolle", BP 21, 16130 Segonzac
Tel: (45) 83 41 73

VSOP (GC) 8 · Réserve (GC) 10 · Vieille Réserve (GC) 15 · Napoléon (GC) · XO (GC)

An old-established family with 57 hectares in the heart of the Grande Champagne, an estate which gives it the opportunity to sell an increasing range of its own, additive-free, cognacs. These are mostly exported to West Germany, the USA, Holland, Denmark and Britain.

TALLEFORT

La Champagne de Saint-Preuil, Saint Preuil, 16130 Segonzac ***Tel: (45) 83 31 99***
VS/XXX 7–9 · VSOP (FC) 8–12 · Napoléon (FC) 12–15 · Vieille Réserve (FC) 16–20 · XO (FC) 20–30 · Hors d'Age (GC) 45–55
Founded four years ago by four growers, Philippe Boujut, Christian Jobit, Christian Fontanaud and Jean-Bernard Millon-Mesnard. Between them they have 100 hectares of vines, 60 in the Grand Champagne, 32 in the Petite Champagne and 8 in the Fins Bois.

The firm is scrupulous about quality: the wines are distilled on light lees to extract the maximum fruitiness; no additives are used; the cognacs are well-aged and kept in small casks only; and the brandies bought in come from growers known personally. Three-quarters of its production goes to the USA.

SIEUR DE PLAISANCE

Guy Testano, Sieur de Plaisance, Lamerac, 16300 Barbezieux ***Tel: (45) 78 04 61***
VSOP 5 · Napoléon 10 · Réserve Hors d'Age 20 · Réserve d'Antan (GC)
Although M. Testano, son and grandson of growers, has 20 hectares in the Champagnes he also buys cognacs, but most of his offerings are from a single *cru*.

TIFFON

29, Quai de l'Ile Madame, 16200 Jarnac ***Tel: (45) 81 08 31***
XXX 7 · VSOP 7–10 · VVO (FC) 12 · Extra (FC) 25
Founded by Mederic Tiffon in 1875. For a long time it specialized in selling in bulk to the Scandinavian monopolies. Since 1946 has been owned by the ubiquitous Braastad family. Tiffon owns two properties, totalling 50 hectares, mostly in the Fins Bois but also in the Grande Champagne – where they grow Folle Blanche as well as Ugni Blanc. Tiffon has six stills of considerable antiquity. Only uses colouring, no other additives.

GERARD TOUZAIN

Rue Millardet, 16130 Segonzac
Reserve (GC) 13
In 1970 M. Touzain inherited 11 hectares in the Grande Champagne. He sells virtually all its output to major Cognac firms, but lays down a few casks of his finest brandies each year to sell to private clients and the occasional passing tourist.

TRADITION BRILLAT-SAVARIN

See Guy de Bersac.

TROIS EMPEREURS

See Guy de Bersac.

TROISGROS

See Jules Robin.

UNICOGNAC

BP2, 17500 Jonzac ***Tel: (46) 48 10 99***
Ansac:
XXX · VSOP · Napoléon · XO
Jules Gautret:
XXX · VSOP · Napoléon · Fine Champagne (FC) · Grande Fine Champagne (FC) · Hors d'Age (FC)
Roi des Rois:
Coronation · VSOP · XO · Hors d'Age

Unicognac is the name of Cognac's cooperative union of 3,500 growers whose 125 stills account for 350,000 hectolitres of cognac a year, enough to fill nine million bottles, and 6% of the region's total production. The 13 stills in its biggest distillery, at La Brousse, alone produces 100,000 hectolitres annually. Its main marque is Prince Hubert de Polignac (qv), but it also has three other brands of its own (as well as supplying large numbers of supermarkets in France and abroad with Buyers Own Brands). Sales are well spread, with Jules Gautret going to Europe and the USA, Roi de Rois to Europe and the Far East, and Ansac all over the world.

ARMAGNAC

The History of Armagnac

Armagnac, as the locals invariably inform even the most casual visitor, is at once the oldest and the youngest spirit in France. Oldest because it was first distilled in the middle of the 15th century, youngest because the Armagnaçais are still arguing over how to distil it. The experimental mood in Armagnac is a welcome contrast to the relative industrial and intellectual stagnation in Cognac.

The region of Armagnac has always been a very special example of that elusive concept, *La France Profonde*, even now well away from the madding crowds – and their motorways. For a thousand years the Armagnaçais have been conscious of themselves as a distinct subgroup. At Auch they say: *"Ici nous somms Gascons. A Eauze ils sont Armagnaçais"* – "Here we are Gascons. At Eauze they are Armagnaçais". Despite their protestations they are essentially Gascons, famous as swaggerers, soldiers *, lovers of rich food (truffles and foie gras) and drink. Their homeland was as near a rural paradise as makes no difference, gentle, fair, fertile countryside as yet unspoilt by any urban sprawls. It is tucked away a hundred miles south of Bordeaux, stretching back from the sands of the Landes through a series of gentle valleys, with none of the grim monoculture which mars other vineyards, but providing the most agreeable type of rustic variety.

That was its attraction – but the corollary was its unsuitability as a production centre for an internationally traded spirit. Armagnac is – sometimes to an exaggerated degree – a reflection of French individuality, while still a deeply united rural community in which the merchants are merely extensions of the growers. Unlike Cognac (or more notably Bordeaux), there has never been a class war in Armagnac; but their individuality produces its own commercial problems. President de Gaulle talked about the problems of a country which made 300 different cheeses. Armagnac has as many individual ways of making brandy. The better-organized Cognaçais, offering a handful of brand names famous for a century or more, have always sold 10 times or more than their southern rivals.

By themselves individualism, change and experiment would not be of any interest if the brandy were not exciting to drink. It is better than that; earthier than cognac, but, at its best, offering a closeness to nature, a depth of fruit and warmth which even the finest cognacs cannot match. Because the Armagnaçais have the choice of three grape varieties and two methods of distillation, the brandy's potential character is enormous.

The History

Rightly, the Armagnaçais pride themselves on a long viticultural history. There have been vines in the region since Roman times. Geographically the name of Armagnac appears for the first time in the middle of the 10th century.

* Alas for the romantically minded, d'Artagnan, the most famous of all Gascons, was mostly employed by the authorities to guard important prisoners.

By the 15th century the English kings had come and gone and for the past 450 years Armagnac (indeed Gascony as a whole) has been a happy country without much history. The most recent devastations, recalled in conversation as though they happened yesterday, swept the region in the 14th or 15th century.

By then wines – and Bayonne, the nearest port, with the unusual freedom to trade in wine – were already important. In the centuries before railways or decent roads trade was largely confined to slopes close to navigable rivers. This created a double problem for the Armagnaçais. In many ways the easiest outlet was the long haul down river to Bordeaux. But right through the Middle Ages the merchants of Bordeaux protected their own wines by refusing to allow the sale of wines from the "Haut Pays", the river basins of the Garonne and the Dordogne, before Christmas of each year. Wines were fragile then, so the ruling – which lasted until well into the 18th century – effectively excluded the wines of Cahors, Bergerac, Montbazillac and Armagnac, from the lucrative British and Dutch trade. The only alternative was to haul the casks by ox cart to the River Midouze for transport to Bayonne, on a river so tricky that it took the local barges three days to travel 38 kilometres.

Distilling the wine at least increased the value of the contents of the casks so laboriously transported. Armagnac had retained a connection with Arabic science in the Middle Ages through the famous University of Montpellier, closely connected with the great Islamic seat of learning at Salerno. It was not surprising that the Armagnaçais learnt the Arab art of distillation before any other French wine-growing district. In 1411, according to a document in the archives of the Haute Garonne, a man called Antoine was distilling wine at Toulouse to obtain *aygue ardente*, also called *aygue de bito*, or eau de vie, literally water of life, a definition which emphasizes that the products of the still were originally used for medicinal purposes. By 1441 a document at Auch records that *"aguza l'entendenem e fa bona memoria e conserva joven e dona gauch e alegrier"*; distilled spirit relieves pain, keeps one young and brings with it joy and relaxation.

The spirit remained a local speciality until the 16th century when the Dutch, in their thirst for *aygue ardente* to supply their ships, were happy to buy Eau de Vie d'Armagnac at Bayonne. After some time it became well-known enough to be called simply armagnac, but was not considered comparable in quality to the brandy from Cognac. Local historians may talk of its international fame, yet armagnac remained a rustic curiosity.

This is something of a puzzle. Like Cognac, Armagnac had a ready supply of acid white wine, and of wood to "burn" it with, a contact with the Dutch to provide a market, and an older indigenous tradition of distillation than cognac. We can still see the earliest known *brûlerie*, set up in the mid-17th century by Thomas de Maniban at his Château de Busca. Moreover, the Manibans were of the *noblesse de la robe*, the legal aristocracy, who cultivated – and sold – the fine wines of Bordeaux so successfully at the time. Yet they, like other Armagnaçais, then as now, lacked the spirit of openness, the commercial aggressiveness, which came naturally to the Cognaçais and their foreign partners, who had built up together a flourishing trade in salt and wine with northern Europe for half a millenium before they distilled their first *brandywijn*. As a result armagnac did not compete as a rival to cognac in the market which counted – the fashionable society of Restoration London. It was probably submerged in the mass of brandies from Bordeaux and "Nants" which were considered inferior to cognac.

By the end of the 17th century armagnac was a well-integrated rural industry. Yet even when the Bordeaux monopoly collapsed during the 18th century it remained largely local because of transport problems. Crucially the River Baise, which empties into the Garonne, was not navigable beyond Port-de-Bordes at Laverac, at the very northern tip of the region. In the first half of the 19th century Armagnac was rescued from its rustic seclusion by two dramatic developments. The first was the invention of the "traditional" Armagnac continuous still, essential for extracting armagnac's particular qualities. The small cognac-type stills used previously were clearly unsuitable for distilling wines from soils as sandy or clayey as those from the best parts of Armagnac – the Ténarèze and the Bas Armagnac. Also, by no means incidentally, the cognac still was too expensive a piece of equipment for the local peasantry. They needed a new simpler type, which was transportable from farmhouse to farmhouse and, above all, much cheaper to heat.

The Continuous Still

The Armagnaçais showed an immediate interest in the continuous still invented by Edouard Adam, their near-neighbour at Montpellier, at the very beginning of the 19th century (their eagerness emphasized the dissatisfaction with the existing apparatus). The idea was first taken up by Antoine de Melet, Marquis de Bonas, a landowner already famous for his new ideas. By 1819 a factory at Eauze was making the new stills, perfected later in the century by a local peasant called Verdier, who gave his name to the final apparatus. Unlke all the other types of continuous stills, the Verdier model retained more of the essential elements in the wine than did the orthodox pot-stills.

This apparatus provided the Armagançais with a raw brandy capable of developing into an even more complex spirit than cognac – albeit at the expense of some initial roughness and woodiness.

The second development was that at the same time the Armagnaçais finally found an economic way of getting their brandies to market. In the late 1830s, after nearly 250 years of discussion, the River Baise was canalled so that the heart of the Ténarèze, if not the Bas-Armagnac, was directly connected with Bordeaux, a world centre for trade in wines and spirits (and no longer with the power to discriminate with tariff barriers). At last the Armagnaçais could market their very special brandies.

By then, unfortunately, the Cognaçais had a 150 year start. Nevertheless, the 50 years after the canal was built witnessed the first real breakthrough into French and, to a certain extent, world markets. Some of today's most famous firms were founded at the time. The first, Castarède, who had been situated at Pont-de-Bordes Lavardac until then, moved with other merchants to Condom, nearer the centre of the region. The boom was real enough; in 1804 the Gers produced 50,000 hectolitres of pure alcohol, a figure which doubled by 1872, by when its 100,000 hectares of vines rivalled the Charente and the Hérault in the competition for the *département* with the biggest area under vines.

Then came a triple disaster familiar to other regions: in the late 1870s mildew arrived, combated a few years later by the sulpher mixture known as *bouilli bordelaise*; black rot followed; then, finally and inevitably, the dreaded phylloxera, which had first been spotted in the region in 1878. Initially it had been kept at bay, partly because it did not flourish in the sandy soils of the Bas Armaganc, finally starting to devastate the region in 1893, ironically a marvellous year for the brandies from the surviving vines.

The devastation was catastrophic, the recovery minimal. The only useful relic of the disaster was the system of Appellation Contrôlée which protected the good name of Armagnac. The classification had been started well before any legal definitions were attempted. In the mid-18th century, the Marquise d'Ivry, born a Maniban, whose husband was the King's chief steward, specified that the royal brandy should come from Cazaubon in the heart of what we now call the Grand Bas Armagnac. In 1850, Jules Seillan published the first *Topographie des Vignobles du Gers et de l'Armagnac* – a work considered so important that it was translated into English. In essence, Seillan, like the scientific pioneers in other parts of France (and indeed the wine brokers who established the 1855 classification in Bordeaux), was codifying on a scientific basis the judgements which the market had already established during the preceding century and before.

In the first decade of the present century, the problem of deciding the legal boundaries of Armagnac and its subdivisions was complicated because Armand Fallières, then President of France, was a native Gascon who owned a property in Armagnac. The Boundary Commission headed by the local prefect decided to follow local custom and divide the area into three, the Bas Armagnac, Ténarèze and Grand Armagnac, each one corresponding to geological, geographical and commercial reality. This confused matters because the best armagnacs come from the apparently lesser appellation, the Bas Armagnac, which many of its supporters thought should be called the Grand Bas Armagnac – Grand Bas is still a term of approbation. The Ténarèze was a vague definition, as vague as the origin of the expression *chemin de crête*, after the stone path which, allegedly, ran from the Pyrenees to Bordeaux without crossing a river.

A leading local merchant, Pierre-Louis Janneau, argued that the success of the Cognaçais was due to having a single appellation only. A sensible compromise was envisaged by a deputation from Riscle near the Pyrenees. It proposed a Grand Bas and two others, Bas Armagnac, and Armagnac in general, which was not accepted, and the three original divisions still rule. The Haut Armagnac, the eastern half of

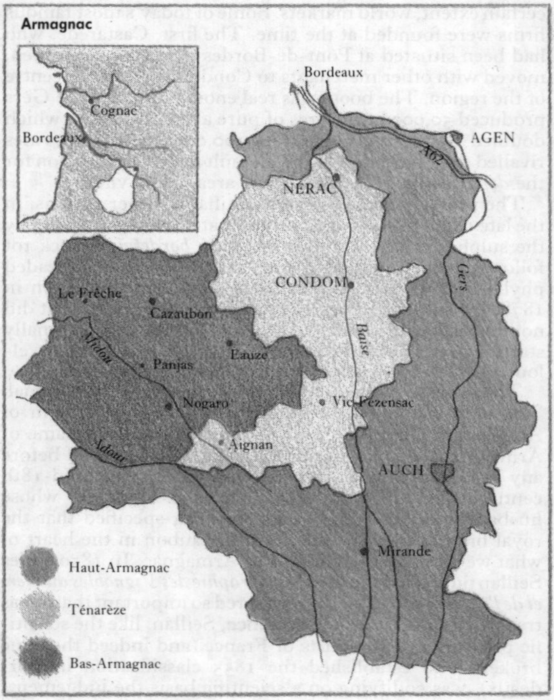

the region, as a producer of brandy never really recovered from the phylloxera (it now specializes in often excellent dry white table wines).

In terms of reputation Armagnac's recovery from the phylloxera took until the 1970s. Cruelly, Armagnac suffered two false dawns. The first, at the end of World War I, was succeeded by a severe slump. By 1937 the region was producing a mere 22,000 hectolitres of spirit, less than a quarter of the pre-phylloxera volume (and even that figure showed an improvement from the depths of the slump).

The end of World War II triggered an even sharper rise and fall. The German occupying forces, largely unaware of the spirit's qualities, had left most of the locals' stocks intact. In 1945 the French people – and American soldiers returning home – found in Armagnac a source of much needed spirit. But the quality was generally poor and, even if it had been better, there was simply no commercial infrastructure to enable the Armagnaçais to exploit their situation. The reaction was swift. Demand slumped so quickly that between 1948 and 1950 virtually no spirit was distilled at all. The growers, short of cash, could not afford to wait for spirit to mature, preferring to sell their grapes as table wine, for which they found a ready welcome.

This provided a major contrast to Cognac, where the local wine is, at best, thin and poor. The Armagnaçais (most obviously in the Haut Armagnac) found that with modern fermentation methods they could make eminently saleable, fruity white wines. This was a major reason behind the continuing slide in the area planted with vines suitable for distillation. Between 1953 and 1965 the total hectarage was reduced by one-third. Today, down to 15,000 hectares, it produces 51,000 hectolitres against the 22,000 from the same area before the last war with a yield three times that of the pre-phylloxera average.

Revival

Despite the reduction in vineyard area, production and demand started to grow in the mid-1960s. This naturally attracted the Cognaçais, anxious to expand from what appeared to be a home base constricted by a lack of sufficient grapes. Martell, Rémy Martin and Camus all took stakes in companies which loomed large on the tiny theatre of Armagnac, although they appeared small to the Cognaçais.

The newcomers were particularly useful in foreign markets. In 1969 only one million out of 2.8 million bottles were exported; by the end of the 1970s half the total, which had risen to eight million, went abroad.

Although Armagnac is outnumbered by twenty to one outside France, it sells one-third as much as its great rival in the domestic market. Unfortunately much of this is cheap, young brandy, for, as life becomes more commercial, more armagnac is sold far too young. Even today the minimum age, a mere two years, is far too low for a traditionally distilled armagnac.

A Cognac pot-still produces a spirit which matures far more rapidly. So with the Cognaçais came their stills. The first cognac-type stills were installed in time for the 1972 harvest, although their cost meant that only a handful of the bigger firms and professional distillers could afford to build them.

To rub in the newcomers' success, disaster overtook the most ambitious local venture, the attempt by a group of cooperatives, the Union de Cooperatives Viticoles de l'Armagnac (UCVA), to establish a major presence. Cooperatives had started just before World War II and had spread in the bad years after the postwar euphoria. But the UCVA was more than merely a defensive response. For a start it was enormous: it embraced 30% of the production, and up to half the total sales of armagnac, including a famous brand name, Marquis de Caussade; but it proved a disaster. The structures were wrong, the management, at best lax, at worst dubious. Brandies were exported without any regard to profit and the money melted away. In 1980 the UCVA went into liquidation and was taken over by its principal creditor, the Crédit Agricole.

Out of the disaster came a useful initiative. Michel Coste, a well-known entrepreneur from Cognac, took over and has used the UCVA stocks to help Armagnac (and, of course, himself). Inevitably the cooperative movement has retreated into the background. Today, although individual cooperatives and their members own 30% of the region's stocks, and a larger proportion of the older armagnacs, they sell only 5% of the total, and none of their brand names is well-known.

The latest worry in Armagnac is the lack of produce from the reduced acreage. This could, however, be good for the region by concentrating attention upon the better grades of armagnac. This is especially important for a spirit, such as armagnac, which is really remarkable only when it has been carefully (and expensively) cherished for several decades. Fortunately there is an increasing demand for the better armagnacs, especially within France. In the world of French gastronomy it has quietly stolen a march on its great rival.

The Personal Touch

The Armagnaçais have two weapons denied to their rivals: the Cognaçais operate on such a large scale that they do not, generally, find it worthwhile to offer brandies from individual estates; and, unlike the Armagnaçais, do not have the legal right to date their brandies.

For the past 20 years every French restaurant worthy of a Michelin star has offered a range of (more or less authentic) single-vintage, single-estate armagnacs. In 1973 Janneau began to market single-vintage armagnacs on a larger scale. "It was our only weapon against the Cognaçais" says Etienne Janneau, "the individual vintages created our image for quality." A few years later the weapon was refined by de Malliac, who started to put the dates of both bottling and distillation on its better products. At a time when every consumer is looking for something special, armagnac is in a far better position than its rival to provide the personal touch.

This emphasis on individual vintages, whose legitimacy depends upon the honesty of the vendors, brings its own dangers. These are being minimized by Armagnac's regulatory authority, the Bureau National Interprofessionel de l'Armagnac (BNIA), set up, like its equivalent in other French wine and spirit regions, after World War II. Jean-Louis Martin, BNIA's shrewd, affable and informal director, does not believe there are important quantities of fraudulent vintages in the market. Any errors, he thinks, are simple human mistakes or (and this practice is obviously almost universal in a region where individual stocks are so small) the result of old vintages being regularly topped up with newer spirits. Only a few firms, like Janneau, have enough stocks of individual vintages to enable them to guarantee the authenticity of every drop of their vintage armagnacs.

Today only armagnacs distilled in years when there were atmospheric nuclear tests can be dated by measuring the level of carbon 14 in the spirit. To guarantee future quality, the BNIA has now ruled that no single vintage can be sold unless it is at least 10 years old; the growers have five years in which to declare the brandies they propose to sell as individual vintages. Not that these differ as much as some authorities pretend; it is possible to find supplies of brandies from almost every year since 1893, the birth year of modern armagnac, when the full impact of phylloxera coincided with a vintage which is still a marvel to drink.

THE LAST TEN YEARS IN ARMAGNAC

Year	Area planted‡	Prod-uction†*	Stocks†	Sales† France	Export	Total	In bottle
1976	21,438	46,833	225,230	21,255	16,869	38,124	53.35%
1977	20,810	12,521	228,780	24,502	19,147	43,649	51.98%
1978	19,688	43,141	205,682	20,146	25,375	45,521	55.20%
1979	21,650	87,154	200,112	21,630	22,425	44,055	56.92%
1980	19,782	35,879	234,581	21,108	19,467	40,575	59.20%
1981	16,592	34,960	227,487	19,425	24,457	43,882	54.80%
1982	15,260	51,215	214,633	19,865	16,838	36,703	66.46%
1983	13,880	33,759	224,298	16,606	14,860	31,482	73.71%
1984	13,611	29,367	220,694	15,666	19,593	35,259	66.87%
1985	12,832	42,708	207,380				

* Vines for distillation only. † In '000hl of pure alcohol. ‡ In hectares.

IDENTIFYING ARMAGNAC

Compte 00,0 cannot by sold
Compte 1,2,3, can be sold only as XXX
Compte 4 can be sold as VO, VSOP, or Réserve
Compte 5 can be sold as Extra, Napoléon, XO and Vieille Réserve
Compte 6 can be sold as any of these names

ARMAGNAC – THE ROOTS OF QUALITY

Unlike almost any other fine wine or spirit, armagnac is a product whose quality derives from sandy soil, albeit of a very particular type. Geologically the region is immensely complicated. It forms part of what was once a deep channel between the older rocks of the Pyrenees and the Massif Central. As the sea ebbed and flowed, it built up irregular layers of sand and clayey rubble from the Pyrenees to the sides of the channel, the region which now forms the Bas Armagnac and the Ténarèze.

The eastern half of the region, the Haut Armagnac, is more orthodox wine-growing country, with chalky slopes reminiscent of Cognac. But, curiously, this is now virtually devoid of vines used for distillation (in 1982 less than 1,000 hectares of vines in the Haut Armagnac produced grapes used for distillation, under 7% of the total). This is not so much because the soil is unsuitable (it is still possible to buy the occasional excellent bottle of Haut Armagnac) but because it has proved simply more profitable for the local growers to turn their Colombard grapes into table wines. The climate is hotter than in Cognac and grapes ripen more fully, although the breezes from the Bay of Biscay ensure the summers never get too hot. The attractions of the landscape are increased by the moist haze through which it is perceived even on the sunniest days.

Nevertheless, today attention is almost exclusively focussed on the western half of the appellation, the Ténarèze and the Bas Armagnac. The soil in the Ténarèze, which combines chalk and clay, results in fine floral armagnacs, reminding connoisseurs unmistakably of violets. By contrast tasters automatically associate the brandies from the Bas Armagnac with plums and prunes, and indeed the best do develop the natural concentrated fruity sweetness of the plum, fresh or dried. The Bas Armagnac is a more complicated area. As the map of the area shows, it is partly in the *département* of the Gers, historically the heart of the Armagnac region, but includes part of the Landes, a *département* associated with sandy pine-covered dunes spreading back from the coast. In the Landes the topsoil is composed of *boulbènes*, an alluvial deposit left by the sea when it finally retreated, covering a subsoil of sand and clay. In the northwest of the Landes the subsoil becomes pure clay, to form a soil known locally as *terre-bouc*. It is this northwest corner which is known and treasured as the Grand Bas, the source of the finest armagnacs. The very best come from the slopes of one of the rare hills in the area, the Catalan, between Laujuzan and Bourrouillan, overlooking the valleys of the rivers Douze and Midour.

The Incomparable Folle Blanche

Historically, the fame of armagnac, like that of cognac, was founded on the flowery aromas emanating from brandies distilled from that incomparable grape the Folle Blanche. The Armagnaçais have their own name for it, the Picpoult (also written Picpoule), although it was introduced into the region only after the Charentais had discovered how suitable it was for distillation purposes. After the phylloxera, in Armagnac as in Cognac, came the discovery that grafting left the Folle Blanche even more susceptible to grey rot than it had been before; and it produced bunches so tightly packed that fungicidal sprays could not reach them. A little Folle Blanche survives and produces brandies – notably one sold by de Malliac – which have a haunting deep, oily, flowery aroma and bouquet. The Armagnaçais have tried to compensate for this loss by planting a little Colombard. This produces some excellent, fruity aromatic brandies (one is sold by André Daguin) but most goes into table wine.

Eighty years after the phylloxera the Armagnaçais were the only Appellation Contrôllée in France to be allowed to use a hybrid, the Baco 22A, a cross of Folle Blanche with the infamous Noah, a grape which produced enormous quantities of bad wine. But in its time the Baco proved immensely useful. In Jancis Robinson's words: "... it ripens late to produce just the sort of low-alcohol, high-acid wine that is perfect for distilling ...". The Baco produces brandy which its friends call sturdy. "*Bien charpenté*" Jacques Pageaux of de Malliac calls them. This is rather polite. It tends to be gross and heavy – a quality much found in older armagnacs which consist almost exclusively of Baco. In these one can also perceive the qualities which made it such a godsend to the stricken Armagnaçais. In the Bas Armagnac, in particular, the Folle Blanche half of its parentage ensures that it can develop full aroma richness typical of an old armagnac.

Since 1945 the vineyard has gradually been taken over by the ubiquitous Ugni Blanc which now accounts for four-fifths of the acreage, with Baco representing 18% and Folle Blanche a mere 2%. Unfortunately, virtually every distiller mixes the varieties in the stills, so only a few varietal Armagnacs are available. Needless to say, those made purely from the Colombard, or, more especially, the Folle Blanche, are well worth tasting.

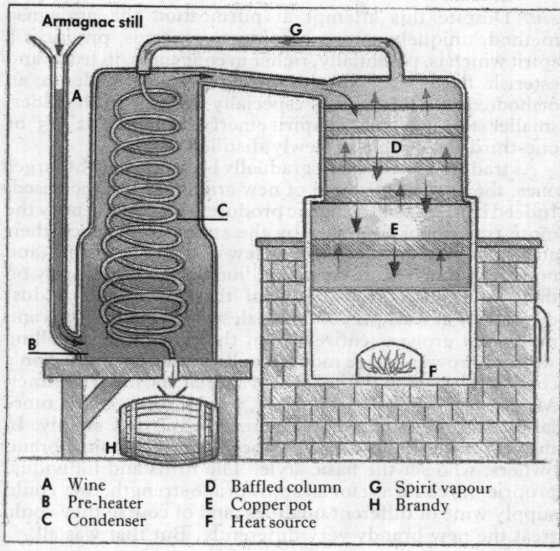

The Methods

As in Cognac, the wine-making is fairly basic, using natural yeasts, eschewing sugar, sulphur dioxide and other additives, a process designed to produce an acceptably neutral raw material for distillation. But there is one crucial difference: the Armagnaçais can use the continuous presses forbidden in Cognac. These, clumsily operated as they too often are, allow through pips, skins and other impurities which further increase the potential richness of the spirit.

This if further assured by the very special type of continuous still developed during the 19th century, and now known as a traditional armagnac still, *à jet continu* – flowing continuously. It was not, of course, the apparatus originally used, but it was the method which made the region's fame and fortune in the middle of the 19th century. The wine is heated in a cylinder (the *chauffe-vin*) by the pipes containing the hot alcoholic vapours from the still. As the diagram on page 77 shows, the wine, by now heated to 80°C, runs into the upper half of a double still. In the old stills the wine flowed to the top, in modern stills the wine enters one or two plates below that point. It then flows over a series of plates, clashing with the alcohol vapours produced by the heated wine in the lower half of the still. The clash allows the vapour to absorb some of the qualities and the congenerics of the incoming wine. The lower the plates the hotter they are, thereby ridding the descending wine of an increasing proportion of its alcohol content as it reaches the lower still, which contains wine boiling at around 103°C.

The *vinasses*, the solid residue of distillation, are evacuated through a pipe in the lower half of the still, the *têtes* can be taken off, as the diagram shows, from the head of the *chauffe-*

vin. Despite this attempt at purification the armagnac method, uniquely among continuous systems, produces a spirit which is, potentially, richer in congeners, in fruity and esterish flavours, than the stronger spirit made in an orthodox pot-still. This is especially the case in the older, smaller stills in which the spirit emerges at a mere 52°, 15° or one-third below that of newly distilled cognac.

As traditional stills have gradually been replaced by larger ones, the average strength of new armagnac has increased. Indeed in the list of armagnac producers one can identify the more traditional suppliers by the strength to which their armagnacs are distilled. Only a few of the larger firms (and none sells much more than a million bottles a year) rely on their own stills for the bulk of their production. Most depend for at least part of their sales – the smaller firms and individual growers entirely – on the remaining travelling stills, the rows of large modern stills owned by the region's cooperatives, or on the handful of specialists, like M. Gimet, M. Lestage and Dr. Garraud, whose names are more familiar in the region than the many firms they supply. In the past it was the distillers, rather than the nominal brand owners, who set the basic style. The firms and individual proprietors could ask for an appropriate strength, they could supply wine of different qualities, and of course they could treat the new brandy very differently. But that was all.

Maturation

Armagnac is such an awkward raw material, needing such careful handling after distillation, that the conditions in which it matures and, above all, the age at which it is sold matter more than for any other brandy. Armagnac made the traditional way may retain more of the character of the original wine, but there is a price to pay. The richness consists of impurities which render the spirit unappetizingly raw for a longer time than spirit distilled by other methods. In the past long maturation was necessary because the old stills were rarely cleaned, which increased the depth (and potential richness) of the impurities in the spirit. A spirit for drinking after less than seven or eight years in wood must be distilled to a much higher degree than is possible in a small, old-fashioned mobile still, whose products are incomparable, but only after a couple of decades.

Unfortunately for armagnac's reputation, it can be sold even younger than cognac, at a mere 18 months of age. And when, in the 1960s and 1970s, the locals started to compete for the French market they relied too heavily on price as a weapon. This in turn meant selling brandies only two or three years old, thus creating a vicious circle. Consumers naturally expected to pay very much less for such an inevitably raw and woody spirit. Hence the pressure which built up in the late 1960s for a change in the regulations, so that the Armagnaçais could use the cognac still which produced brandies saleable at a mere two or three years of age. When permission was finally granted in 1972 a few of the larger distillers and a number of the larger firms (including Janneau and Sempé) installed cognac stills. It soon became clear that, as they had hoped, the cognac method was perfectly suitable for armagnacs destined to be sold young. But everyone was wary of using them other than for their cheaper brands and the jury is still out on the final verdict. A mere 14 years is not long enough to judge whether armagnac distilled *à la Charentaise* will mature into a spirit as interesting as that produced by the traditional method. A 1975 distilled *à La Charentaise* I tasted had a lovely light nose, with all the floweriness of the best armagnac, but was rather harsh on the palate, short, not as complex as the "real thing". But this could be accidental, a 1973 tasted at de Malliac was developing nicely into an orthodox armagnac, very similar to one distilled by the traditional method.

Old and New Styles

The stylistic variation resulting from the two distillation methods has inevitably confused some customers. The Scandinavians, good clients for the cheaper armagnacs, reject the new-style spirits, they like the old-style armagnac, so obviously different from cognac. The French (the connoisseurs, rather than the buyers of the basic young spirit) also prefer the heavier, traditional, armagnacs, while many British buyers – there are only a few true armagnac aficionados in Britain – have come to like the lighter "cognacised" spirit.

The existence of a rival system has spurred the traditional distillers into finding ways of improving their old formulae. The first problem was to reduce the *queues*, the heavy low-strength, aroma-heavy products. They can be filtered out at a specific point on the distillation column, reduced by introducing a condenser above the still, or two more plates within the still above the level at which the wine flows in from the *chauffe-vin*. M. Lestage has adapted the traditional still to eliminate some of the esters by trapping them in a pierced copper plate at the top of the still. All these adjustments, combined with increasing the strength of the new armagnac to between 66 and 68°, close to that of raw cognac, reduce the quintessential richness of the spirit, but they do make it more commercial; it can be sold as a quality product after seven or eight years, rather than after 20.

Experimental Stills

The most promising investigations have been carried out by Dr. Garraud in his experimental stills. In one experiment, in conjunction with de Malliac, he has succeeded in getting rid of the aggressive esters by diverting the *queues* and remixing them with the wine. In these and other experiments he has achieved a balance between the two systems, eliminating some of the *queues* while retaining the essential elements within them.

The underlying depth – some would call it heaviness – of armagnac comes from a combination of soil, grape varieties (especially the Baco) and the retention of the fruity *secondes*. Clearly the use of oak casks, traditionally from the local forest of Monlezun, has emphasized these qualities. Recently the shortage of local Gascon oak has forced most growers and firms to use casks made from the same Tronçais and the Limousin as the Cognaçais. This has led to a lot of head-shaking in Armagnac. But analyses show, as might be expected, there is no great chemical difference between the three types. Although no one is quite sure what long-term immersion in non-Gascon oak will do to the spirit, Étienne Janneau, for one, takes the robust commonsense view that: "the *terroir* will always come through".

In its first year the newly distilled spirit is usually stored in traditional 400 litre casks, just under the roof of the warehouse, where the temperature varies more, and the air circulates more freely than it would nearer the floor. This accelerates the process of oxidization before the casks are brought down to the stabler conditions at floor level. At de Malliac's they give the newly distilled spirit a quick fix of tannin by keeping it in new oak for up to a year. It is then invariably transfered to old wood to assimilate the tannin, and to ensure that it does not get an overdose. For reasons which the locals take for granted, but find difficult to explain, the alcoholic strength of traditionally distilled armagnacs diminishes more slowly in cask than does cognac.

The actual process of maturation is, of course, parallel to that for cognac. However, the character of the final spirit depends less on the vanillin and lignin in the wood, than it does on the more neutral spirit from Cognac; the *terroir*, the warmth, the fruity, almost herbal earthiness comes through more strongly in armagnac – reducing the importance of the *rancio* which is so necessary in old cognacs. Unfortunately, so too does the woodiness. Because armagnac was a peasant-based industry the growers tended to keep their spirits in wood far too long, right up to the moment of bottling – usually in traditional bottles *à la Basquaise*, supposedly modelled upon the historic shape of goat-skins. Consequently, very old armagnacs, left in the cask for 50 years or more, can be exceedingly woody.

But that is a somewhat esoteric consideration for the average buyer of armagnac. They should abjure the cheaper spirits altogether, buying nothing below eight or 10 years old, and then only from the handful of firms – such as Janneau, de Maillac, and, nowadays, Sempé – who are big enough to provide a proper house style. However, only a spirit with 20 years or more in cask can provide the essence of that spirit. These armagnacs will usually be sold with a vintage date on them, because they fetch a higher price than when sold as a blend. Above the 20-year XO level (where there are some excellent commercial blends to be found) the buyer can rely only on the shipper or the domaine from which the spirit comes.

The actual year seems (and I know this sounds heretical) not overly relevant. Although a number of authorities provide long lists of supposedly superior vintages (invariably, and justifiably, starting with the 1893), there are enough armagnacs from almost every year available from reputable estates to suggest there is less difference between the years than the locals make out. A well-cherished cask of a supposedly mediocre year can be superb, better than the carelessly handled product of an allegedly vintage harvest. For this is one of the joys of armagnac. It is the least industrial of the great spirits, the one where amateurs can most legitimately hope to find a little-known bottle which they can cherish because it offers unique qualities not found even in the next cask in the cellar from which it came.

ARMAGNAC

· DIRECTORY ·

It is impossible to provide a comprehensive list of available armagnacs since virtually every grower sells at least a part of his production directly. I have confined the list to firms which offer a full range, and to growers who offer an above average quality of armagnac with stocks substantial enough to maintain sales and quality. Many armagnacs from individual estates are sold through firms such as Darroze which specialize in single-vineyard armagnacs. The directory is in alphabetical order listing brand names, not the firms or individuals owning them (although I have provided cross-references where the owner is well-known). The years given for single-vintage armagnacs are those available at the time of going to press.

Entries on many individual estates owe a great deal to the *Guide de L'Amateur d'Armagnac* by Fernand Cousteaux and Pierre Casamayor.

Unless otherwise indicated, the firms welcome visitors if forewarned.

Armagnacs coming from specific regions are indicated as follows:

BA exclusively from Bas Armagnac.
T exclusively from the Ténarèze
HA exclusively from the Haut Armagnac

PHILIPPE AURIAN

32100 Condom en Armagnac ***Tel: (62) 28 13 29***
M. Aurian's cellars at Domaine de Thomas, Lannes, 47170 Mezin ***Tel: (53) 65 71 65***
XXX (T) · VSOP (T) · Hors d'Age (T) · Napoléon (T) · Extra Vieux (T) · XO (T)
Visits: Any time without appointment

Founded in 1900 by a M. Dupeyron, a grower who started to sell his armagnacs that year at the Universal Exhibition in Paris. His son was killed in World War I, but the family business was continued by his son-in-law, René Aurian, a broker and wholesaler in wine and armagnac. His son Jean took over in 1952 and began to sell under the family name.

Jean and Philippe Aurian own 14 hectares of Ugni Blanc and Colombard at the Domaine de Thomas. They also buy 50,000 hectolitres of wine from small growers around Condom which they distil in their two postwar stills to produce 10 hectolitres a day. The Aurians specialize in armagnacs from the Ténarèze which are lighter and less aggressive if the wine is distilled to 68 to 71°. They can then be sold within six years of distillation. Their XO has a splendid fresh, vanilla nose, rich on the palate, caramelly, and a bit oily. The Hors d'Age has a similar nose but is finer on the palate, more elegant and has more bite.

AUXIL

Fatima Brothers, 40230 St-Georges-de-Marsan
Tel: (58) 57 30 40

An extraordinary Christian brotherhood whose ministry

seemingly consists of providing the finest of food and drink. They own fine restaurants, listing a range of single malt whiskies and a number of single-vineyard, single-vintage armagnacs, offered at their natural strength, and therefore changing as supplies are extended.

BARON DE GASCONNY

see St Vivant.

LA BOUBEE

Jean Ladevèze La Boubée, 52250 Montréal-du-Gers *Tel: (62) 28 41 85* (Also owns La Salle-Puissant) Vintages: 1942–84

A family property of 20 hectares producing armagnac since 1882. It is one of the regrettably rare estates where the old varieties Plant de Graisse and Jurançon are cultivated (as well as Ugni Blanc and Colombard).

M. Gimet distils the wines for the firm both traditionally and *à la Cognaçaise*, keeping them in new local oak for up to 18 months. The firm keeps stocks of 300 hectolitres; it wins numerous prizes.

AU BOURDIEU

M. Joel Fourteau, Au Bourdieu Lauraët, 32610 Mouchan *Tel: (62) 28 41 37*

M. Fourteau distils the Colombard and Ugni Blanc from his 14 hectare estate himself to a mere 53%, and then keeps them for a year in new local wood. Over the past 10 years he has built up stocks of 500 hectolitres and sells them at their natural strength.

BRILLAT SAVARIN

Tradition Brillat Savarin, 60 Avenue de la Bourdonnais, 75007 Paris *Tel: (1 45) 56 12 20* Fine 3–5 · VSOP 8 · Hors d'Age 12–15 · Millésime 20 · Grande Réserve 25 · Domaine du Chillot

Subsidiary of an important French drinks marketing group which also owns Guy de Bersac Cognac (qv). No vineyards of its own but buys in a lot of Folle Blanche and Baco to feed its two traditional stills. These produce 1,500 hectolitres of pure alcohol a year. The firm sells nearly 50,000 bottles a year abroad.

CACHET DU ROI

M. Lefebure, Domaine du Have, Ste-Christie-D'Armagnac, 32370 Manciet

M. Lefebure's 22 hectares of Colombard and Ugni Blanc are traditionally distilled and kept in new wood for nine months. Stocks of about 1,000 hectolitres.

CARBONNEL

See St Vivant.

CASSOUS

See Le Tastet.

CASTAIGNE

See St Vivant.

CASTARÈDE

Pont-de-Bordes, 47230 Lavardac ***Tel: (53) 65 50 06***
VSOP · Numerous single vintages (BA) · Domaine de Maniban VSOP (BA) · Nismes-Delclou

Naturally proud of being the oldest business in Armagnac. Founded in 1832 by Jules Nismes at the suggestion of a young subprefect, who later became famous as the Baron Haussmann who replanned Paris for the Emperor Napoléon III. The firm was sited at the furthest point to which the Boise is navigable and provides direct access to Bordeaux down the River Garonne.

The firm is still owned by the Castarède family, who are also proprietors of the picturesque Château de Maniban at Mauleon d'Armagnac. The Maniban family were members of the legal aristocracy, the *noblesse de la Robe*, which played such an important role in developing Bordeaux's fine wine estates. They were the first to introduce armagnac to the court of Louis XV. (*See* Château du Busca-Maniban.)

The firm offers a VSOP but the sales (of around 100,000 bottles annually) are concentrated on individual vintages, sold not only under the firm's name, but also to numerous selective buyers like the Fouquets, Hédiard and Berry Bros Batailley.

The firm is not a distiller; it buys armagnacs, exclusively from the Bas Armagnac, distilled between 1900 and 1976, keeps them in wood only until they have naturally reduced to 40% and then transfers them to glass *bonbonnes*. Its single vintages are sold at natural strength, without additives; and the quality: "they have the same characteristics, even if they are inevitably different" says Florence Castarède, a necessarily enigmatic answer given the diverse origins of the firm's products.

CASTEJA

Borie-Manoux, 86 Cours Balguerie-Stuttenberg, 33082 Bordeaux ***Tel: (56) 48 57 57***
XXX 5 · VSOP Spéciale 7–8 · VSOP Grande Réserve 10–12 · Hors d'Age 15–25. Vintages: 1964 and 1959

Borie-Manoux is a well-known Bordeaux wine merchant's, run by M. Emile Castéja, who also owns Château Haut-Batailley.

A delightful if peppery fellow with very high standards, M. Castéja loved armagnac but was dissatisfied with the quality available. So he set up his own business, based in an 18th century farmyard at Courransan. His armagnacs are virtually all continuously distilled. Most come from the Bas-Armagnac, with a little from Ténarèze, bought either from individual distillers or from the Armagnac exchange. He eschews additives, using only a little treacle to deepen the colour.

CASTELFORT

See Vignerons d'Armagnac.

CAUSSADE

See Marquis de Caussade.

CHABOT
Compagnie Viticole des Grands Armagnacs, Route de Bordeaux, BP 8, 40190 Villeneuve de Marsan
Tel: (58) 45 21 76
Head Office:
29 Rue Marguerite de Navarre, BP19, 16101 Cognac ***Tel: (45) 32 28 28***
Chabot: Blason d'Or · Napoléon · XO · Extra
Gerland: XXX · VSOP · Napoléon
St Michel: XXX · VSOP · Napoléon
Marquis de Puysegur: XXX · VSOP · Sélection privée · 20 Ans d'Age · single vintages
The group started as Gerland, a cooperative in the Bas Armagnac. It now embraces a great number of brands, including single-estate armagnacs, all under the umbrella of Camus, the cognac company which owns the marketing company CGVA and the principal brands, Chabot and Marquis de Puysegur. Thanks to the Camus marketing clout, these are the biggest sellers outside France. CGVA owns 60 hectares of Ugni Blanc at Esplavais near Eauze in the Bas Armagnac, and uses the brandy, which it distils in its own traditional still, in their blends.

CHATEAU D'ASTERAC
See Marquis de Montesquieu.

CHATEAU DU BUSCA-MANIBAN
Mme Jacqueline Palthey de Roll, Sté Vinicole de Busca-Maniban, 32310 Masencome
Tel: (62) 29 12 02
Vintages: 1940, 1950, 1964, 1968
The château was built in the 17th century for a well-known local family, the Manibans (*See* Castarède). The Manibans were distilling as the château was being built. Indeed a still-house near the château may be the oldest in the region.

The present owner, a descendant of the family, has the Ugni Blanc and Colombard from the estate distilled traditionally by Bernès and kept in new local wood for up to two years.

CHATEAU DE CASSAIGNE
Henri Faget, Château de Cassaigne, 32100 Condom
Tel: (62) 28 04 02
The château, owned by the family for seven generations, was once the home of the Bishops of Condom. The still-house dates from the 18th century, although the grapes from M. Faget's 27 hectares of Colombard and Ugni Blanc are now distilled by M. Bernès. His stocks of 850 hectolitres have been stored in new local oak for two years.

CHATEAU DE LABALLE
M. Laudet, Château de Laballe, Parlebosc, 40310 Gabarret ***Tel: (58) 44 32 03***
Vintages: (BA) 1963–83
Bought by M. Laudet's ancestor in 1820 with the proceeds from the sale of the ship in which he had returned from the West Indies. The estate, of 11 hectares, is planted exclusive-

ly with Ugni Blanc and Colombard. Distilled by Dargelos and kept in new local wood for four years.

CHATEAU DE LACAZE

Christopher Oldham, Château de Lacaze, Parleboscq en Armagnac, 40310 Gabarret
Tel: (58) 44 33 65
Chateau de Lacaze · Heritage · Marquis de Lasserre

One of the two British pioneers in Armagnac. At the very north of the Bas Armagnac, the estate, of 60 hectares planted with the four classic varieties, surrounds a magnificent, beautifully restored, medieval château. Christopher Oldham takes enormous care over every stage in making his armagnac. The varieties are vinified, distilled and aged separately. The grapes are cold-fermented using selected yeasts. Oldham has a relatively small, new still and has some wine distilled by the enterprising M. Lestage. The new armagnac is matured for up to 11 months in new oak casks, using different types for each variety (the Allier for Ugni Blanc and Folle Blanche, the Limousin for Colombard and Ugni Blanc, and local oak for the Baco). When mature it is reduced in six stages by *petits eaux* of 17%.

Oldham combines tradition and new marketing techniques. He sells the newly distilled armagnac to buyers in Britain whose names remain on the casks. He thus avoids financing charges while spreading the armagnac gospel to a class of Britons who normally associate fine brandy exclusively with cognac.

CHATEAU DE LACQUY

Jean de Boissesson, Château de Lacquy, 40190 Lacquy ***Tel: (58) 44 80 82***
Vintages: (BA) 1972–74

Historic estate in the far west of the Armagnac region which has been in the same family since 1711. Over the past 20 years M. de Boissesson has built up stocks of 320 hectolitres of armagnacs from a small (12 hectare) estate. They are distilled to 53% and stored in 19th century cellars, after one to three years in new local oak.

CHATEAU DE LAUBADE

M. Jean-Jacques Lesgourgues, GFA de Laubade, Sorbets, 32110 Nogaro ***Tel: (62) 09 06 02***
VSOP (BA) 6 · XO (BA) 8 · Vintages: 1974–75 · (also 22 vintages from 1895–1965 not from the estate)

In 1974 the estate of 100 hectares surrounding the 19th century château was bought by M. Lesgourgues, director of a seed merchant's. A successful pioneer in introducing fine single-estate armagnacs to a wider public, he distils his own spirit and keeps it in new oak from Montlezun for three years.

CHATEAU DE MALLIAC

See J. de Malliac.

CHATEAU DE MANIBAN

See Castarède.

CHATEAU DE POMES-PEBERERE

Louis Faget, Château de Pomes-Peberère, 32100 Condom *Tel: (62) 28 11 53*
(T) 5, 10 and 20

M. Louis Faget is a well-known viticulturist, inventor of the system of pruning which bears his name. The family has owned the 35 hectare estate for 150 years and M. Faget makes armagnacs in his own unique style from vines which are purely Ugni Blanc and Colombard. He distils them himself, does not use any new oak and keeps his stocks of 900 hectolitres in casks from Allier, Limousin and Gascony.

CHATEAU DE SANDEMAIGNAN

Sté Thermale de Barbotan, 32150 Cazaubon
Tel: (62) 09 55 92
Vintages: 1966–84 (except 1978)

Estate of 52 hectares owned by the famous restaurateur Michel Guérard. Previously owned for centuries by the Caffins, a distinguished local family. The vineyard has been replanted during the past 20 years with Colombard, Ugni Blanc and Folle Blanche, distilled in the classic fashion and kept in new Tronçais oak for up to one year. Sold as individual vintages only, at natural strength for the French market, reduced to 43% for export. Sold exclusively at the estate or through M. Guérard's restaurant at Eugenie-les Bains.

CHATEAU DE TARIQUET

P. Grassa et Fils, Château de Tariquet, 32800 Eauze
Tel: (62) 09 87 82
XXX (BA) 3 · VSOP (BA) 6–7 · Hors d'Age (BA) 12–15

A well-regarded, traditional and substantial estate of 60 hectares with mixed varieties of grape (including some Baco). Each variety is distilled separately and traditionally over a wood fire, then kept in new local oak for up to 15 months. Stocks of 2,500 hectolitres. M. Grassa's armagnacs, reduced by *petites eaux*, have won numerous prizes.

LE CHEVALIER GASCON

32800 Eauze *Tel: (62) 09 80 60*
XXX · VSOP · Hors d'Age · Vintages 1941–62

A major cooperative at Eauze, grouping 400 growers with 1,100 hectares of vines. Nearly half are Baco. Large producers both of armagnac and table wine. Uses five classic stills and oak casks from the Tronçais for stocks of 8,300 hectolitres.

CLEF DES DUCS

64107 Bayonne *Tel: (59) 55 09 45*
XX · VSOP · 15 · 21

A major firm, owned by Izarra and distributed by its parent company, Cointreau. It has a carefully thought-out policy to ensure it can sell its armagnacs young (although it does hold substantial stocks of old armagnacs in a humidity controlled cellar). The wines are preselected, distilled largely by cooperatives and housed in wood from the Allier – less tannic than from other regions. They are diluted with *petites eaux* of 30% made from strong armagnac from the Ténarèze. Unfortunately, despite these precautions (or perhaps because of them), the younger armagnacs rather lack character.

COMTE DE GUYON

Baronne H. de Guyon de Pampelonne, Château de Lassalle, Maupas en Armagnac, 32240 Estang
***Tel: (62) 09 63 09.* Paris Office Tel: (1 47) 27 95 30**
Hors d'Age (BA) 44% 9–10 · also various vintages from 1942 to 1975 (BA)
A traditional family property of 20 hectares in the heart of the Bas Armagnac, mostly planted with Ugni Blanc.

COMTE DE LAFITTE

See Larresingle.

PIERRE CORNET

See Plachat.

LA CROIX DE SALLES

H. Dartigalongue et Fils, BP 9, 32110 Nogaro
Tel: (62) 09 03 01
XXX · VSOP · Napoléon · Tresor de Famille 15–20 · Réserve Extra Vieille · Vintages: 1944–64
Old and highly respected firm, founded in 1838 by Pascal Dartigalongue. In 1870 his son bought a major estate at Salles-d'Armagnac and named the armagnacs after it. The firm is now run by the fifth generation of his family. They own two classic stills, using only brandies from the Bas Armagnac. In 1972 they installed four Cognac stills to provide brandy for their younger offerings.

CYRANO

M. Bats, Cadets de Gascogne, 40000 Mont-de-Marsan *Tel: (58) 75 26 10*
XXX · VSOP 7–8 · VSOP 10 · 10 Ans (45%) · Hors d'Age 17–18 · Hors d'Age 20 (also at 45%) · Single vintage armagnacs from 1893–1969 at natural strength
Founded in 1922, the firm has changed hands several times recently. Owned for a time by some Swiss who were more interested in bottling the fruits of Armagnac than in the brandy. Fortunately in 1979 it was bought back by M. Bats, a grandson of one of the founders, who now runs it with his son. Very good stock of old armagnacs.

ANDRE DAGUIN

Hotel de France, Place de la Liberation, 32000 Auch *Tel: (62) 05 00 44*
Daguin: Haut Armagnac 20 · Ténarèze (T) 45% 20 · Bas Armagnac (BA) 43% 24
Marquis de Terraube: (HA) 46 · 4% 20
André Daguin is the high priest of local gastronomy, inventor of Magret de Canard, and a specialist in many a delicious, liverish concoction made from the local geese. He deliberately disdains fashion, buying small lots from specially chosen individual growers and selling armagnacs from

all three subregions. He specializes in Ténarèze but has even found some excellent Haut Armagnac near Lectoure.

DAMBLAT

32240 Castelnau d'Auzan ***Tel: (62) 29 21 11/22***
XXX 2–3 · Napoléon 5 · Vieille Réserve 10 · Various vintages
Visits: Every day except Sundays and holidays 10 a.m.–1 p.m. and 2–5 p.m.
Traditional family firm. Founded in 1859 by a grower, Jean Damblat. The family now owns major estates, and uses only armagnac stills. It keeps its armagnacs in new wood for five to seven years and holds extensive stocks.

DANFLOU

See Marquis de Montesquieu.

DARROZE

Bas-Armagnac Francis Darroze, Route de St Justin, 40120 Roquefort ***Tel: (58) 45 51 22***
Sells only under the name of individual domaines. Francis Darroze is the son of a famous restaurateur who made his restaurant in Villeneuve-de-Marsan a place of gastronomic pilgrimage. Since 1974 his son has appointed himself the "antiquary of Armagnac" dedicated to the discovery and sale of dozens of armagnacs distilled in small properties. His rules are strict: he buys only in the Bas Armagnac; the armagnac must have been distilled in the traditional fashion; he never (*un grand jamais*) allows any form of additive to be used. The casks are made only from local wood, air-dried for five years, then fashioned by a *tonnellier* under M. Darroze's supervision.

The armagnacs are stored either where they were distilled or in one of M. Darroze's two cellars, the lower one damp, with an earth floor, the upper one dry. They are left in new wood for two to five years, depending on the quality of the wood, then racked and further matured in old woods. They are aerated every two years to help oxidization and sold (sometime after their twelfth birthday) in their natural state under the name of their original *terroir*. The bottles are marked not only with the year of distillation but also the date of bottling.

M. Darroze's obsession is now a thriving business. He finances dozens of proprietors, paying the costs of distillation, casks and storage, thus keeping them in business. He has also built up the good name of armagnac by demonstrating the range and quality available.

DARTIGALONGUE

See Croix de Salles.

DE MONTAL

For full details *see* Montal.
Compagnie des Produits de Gascogne, 32000 Auch
Tel: (62) 08 81 81
VSOP 8+ · Réserve 12+ · Vintages: Cazaubon 1893–1943 · Panjas 1925–55 · Grand Bas Armagnac 1941 · Eauze 1960, 1961 · Ténarèze 1958, 1962

DOMAINE D'AULA
Patrick Aurin, Domaine d'Aula, 32100 Condom
Tel: (62) 28 12 98
Vintages: 1944–73
Substantial (50 hectares) estate planted only with Colombard and Ugni Blanc. It sells spirits distilled traditionally and kept in new local wood for a year.

DOMAINE BALENTON
See Le Roy des Armagnacs.

DOMAINE DE BOINGNERES
Léon Lafitte, Domaine de Boingnères, Le Frèche, 40190 Villeneuve-de-Marsan ***Tel: (58) 45 24 05***
Vintages: from 1959 onwards
M. Lafitte has 19 hectares in the very heart of the Bas Armagnac planted with Mauzac as well as the four classic varieties. A passionate traditionalist and defender of the Folle Blanche (and who can blame him?). He uses his own still to produce low-degree spirits, housing them in new local oak for two years or more.

DOMAINE DE CAVAILLON
Dr A. Pitous, Domaine de Cavaillon, Lagrange, 40240 Labastide d'Armagnac ***Tel: (58) 44 81 34***
Vintages: (BA) 1893 etc
Dr Pitous is a well-known personality in the Bas Armagnac, selling vintages from his 18 hectare estate, planted with all four classic varieties, distilled by Dargelos and stored in new oak from the estate.

DOMAINE DU CHILLOT
See Brillat-Savarin.

DOMAINE D'ESCOUBES
M. Gérard Laberdolive, Domaine d'Escoubes, 40240 Labastide d'Armagnac ***Tel: (58) 44 81 32***
Vintages: (BA) from 1904 onwards
(Also sells Domaines de Jaurrey, de Pillon, de Labrune)
M. Gérard Laberdolive has worthily continued his father's pioneering efforts to sell single-vintage, single-vineyard armagnacs. His small home-estate houses an old-style still; the armagnacs are matured in oak from the estate. They are stocked by many of the best French restaurants. He does not welcome casual, amateur visitors.

DOMAINE DE GAYROSSE
Dr Charles Garraud, Domaine de Gayrosse, 40240 Labastide d'Armagnac ***Tel: (58) 44 81 08***
Vintages: (BA) from 1928 onwards
As can be seen from the section on new techniques, Dr Garraud is a restless innovator who invented that "traditional" drink, Floc de Gascogne. His family has owned the estate since 1919, and on his 21 hectares he can combine all his enthusiasms. He grows all four classic varieties, distils them in his own specially adapted stills (which form part of his school for distillers) and houses them in casks made from

oaks grown on the estate. He also owns (and shows proudly to the public) an armagnac museum.

DOMAINE DU HAVE

See Cachet du Roi.

DOMAINE DE JAURREY

See Domaine d'Escoubes.

DOMAINE DE LABRUNE

See Domaine d'Escoubes.

DOMAINE DE LAHITTE

See Ferte de Parthenay.

DOMAINE LES LANNES

Christian Domange, Domaine Les Lannes, 32310 Bezolles ***Tel: (62) 28 55 67***
VSOP (T) · Hors d'Age (T)
A 12 hectare estate lovingly restored by M. Domange over the past 12 years. He has his wine (exclusively Ugni Blanc) distilled traditionally and keeps it for one year in new oak.

DOMAINE DE LASSAUBATJU

M. Blondeau, Domaine de Lassaubatju, Hontanx, 40190 Villeneuve-de-Marsan ***Tel: (58) 45 23 01***
Vintages: (BA) 1962–79
Well-known small estate (only 5 hectares) in the Bas-Armagnac, which has been in the hands of the same family since time immemorial. Classic style: Baco and Ugni Blanc, distilled to a mere 52% by Dargelos and kept in new local wood for one to two years.

DOMAINE DE MANIBAN

See Castarède.

DOMAINE DE MARIGNAN

Famille Monnoyeur, Laas, 32170 Mielan
VSOP (HA) · Hors d'Age (HA)
Small (5 hectare) estate with stocks of nearly 600 hectolitres. In the totally unfashionable Haut Armagnac yet wins prizes for its classic armagnacs distilled by the cooperative at Vic-Fezensac and kept for a year in new local oak.

DOMAINE DE MAUPAS

M. Buffaumène, Domaine de Maupas, Mauleon d'Armagnac, 32240 Estang ***Tel: (62) 09 65 02***
Vintages: From 1932 onwards
Classic 30 hectare estate with decent (230 hectolitre) stocks of armagnacs made from all four classic varieties, distilled (by Cornet) to 53%, housed for six months in new local oak.

DOMAINE DE MIQUER

M. Lasserre, Domaine de Miquer, Hontanx, 40190 Villeneuve-de-Marsan
Vintages: (BA) 1964–78
Small (8 hectare) estate of Ugni Blanc, Baco and Folle Blanche. M. Lasserre has his own classic still, producing

armagnac at 53% which is left in new wood (Limousin and local) for two to three years. Sells his brandies at natural strength. Stocks of 260 hectolitres.

DOMAINE DE MOUCHAC

See Janneau.

DOMAINE D'OGNOAS

Arthez d'Armagnac, 40190 Villeneuve-de-Marsan ***Tel: (58) 45 22 11***

Estate of 24 hectares owned by the *département* of the Landes. Supposedly a showpiece for the region. The estate is mostly planted with Ugni Blanc, although it retains some Baco. Historic 180 year-old still, distilling only to 52%.

DOMAINE DE PAPOLLE

Peter Hawkins, Domaine de Papolle, Mauleon d'Armagnac, 32240 Estang ***Tel: (62) 09 62 85***
VSOP (BA) 4+ · Hors d'Age (BA) 7+; Vintages: (BA) 1962, 1965, 1969

One of the two British estate owners, Peter Hawkins has 45 hectares in the Bas Armagnac, planted with Ugni Blanc, Colombard and Folle Blanche over the past 30 years. The brandy is distilled for him by Dargelos to 55%, kept in new local oak for nine months. Has built up stocks of 700 hectolitres.

DOMAINE DE PERE

M. Dufrechou, Bourrouillan, 32370 Manciet
10 · Vintages: 1928–84, natural strength

Estate of 32 hectares, which has been exploited by the Dufrechou family since the days of King Louis XI at the end of the 15th century. Mix of vines, with Ugni Blanc, Colombard, some old Baco. His armagnacs are distilled by M. Lestage, then stored for up to two years in new oak.

DOMAINE DE PILLON

See Domaine d'Escoubes.

DOMAINE DE RAVIGNAN

Baron de Ravignan, Perquié, 40190 Villeneuve-de-Marsan ***Tel: (58) 45 22 04***
Vintages: (BA) every year since 1967

Well-known 18 hectare estate in the Bas-Armagnac planted with the four classic varieties, distilled by Roumat to 52%. The spirit is kept in new local wood for up to 18 months and sold at its natural strength. Frequent prize-winner.

DUCASTAING

See St Vivant.

DUC D'EJAS

32110 Nogaro

Major cooperative with 2,564 members averaging 2.38 hectares of vines each, all round Panjas, a region much prized for its Bas Armagnacs. They use only classic stills and local wood to hold their considerable stocks of 20,000 hectolitres.

DUPEYRON

Ryst Dupeyron, 1 Rue Daunou, 32100 Condom
Tel: (62) 28 08 08
Spéciale Cuisine 4 · VSOP 7–17 · Napoléon 10–25 · XO 20–50

Old-fashioned family firm, founded by M. J. Dupeyron in time to win a medal at the 1900 Paris Universal Exhibition for armagnacs. Their style has not greatly changed since then. The firm is now owned and run by M. Dupeyron's grandson, Jacques Ryst. In the classic fashion M. Ryst buys his wine himself (70% in the Bas Armagnac, 30% in the Ténarèze), all of it Folle Blanche, and has it distilled by an outside distiller who owns four modern armagnac stills. He also buys from small growers.

Dupeyron's fine 18th century private house in Condom provides ample cellarage for his considerable stocks – M. Ryst also sells single vintages to private clients and to members of the Club Vintage which he has built up. He takes particular care when reducing his armagnacs, which is carried out in up to eight stages, using pure mountain water from the Pyrenees, leaving one to two years for the mixture to mature.

M. Ryst adds sugar syrup to his armagnacs, which he reckons to be more supple and perfumed, lighter and less tannic, than the average.

LOUIS FAGET

See Château de Pomes-Peberère.

FERTE DE PARTHENAY

Magnan, 32110 Nogaro ***Tel: (62) 09 02 50***
Domaine de Lahitte (BA) 1973–74. Vintages: 1924–75

Specializes in buying and marketing, especially in Japan and Switzerland, rare old single-vintage armagnacs, sold at their natural strength.

GELAS

BP 3, 32190 Vic-Fezensac ***Tel: (62) 06 30 11***
Selection 5 · VSOP 10–12 · Hors d'Age 20–25

Very traditional family business, founded in 1865 by Baptiste Gélas, the grandfather of Pierre Gélas, the present owner, whose sons Bertrand and Philippe now work with him. The family owns (and Bertrand runs) the Château de Martet at Mancet in the Bas Armagnac with 50 hectares of vines, 80% Ugni Blanc, the rest Folle Blanche. These account for 15 to 20% of the firm's requirements.

Tradition does not prevent Gélas from harvesting by machine - though yields are kept deliberately low. The wines are distilled in two ancient stills, one mobile holding 10 hectolitres, the other fixed, double the volume.

While still on their lees the wines are distilled as soon as possible after fermentation, in the old style – to a mere 52% – the brandy is then kept in new local wood until bottled. Gélas also sells numerous classic single-vintage Bas Armagnacs.

GIMET

See Le Roy des Armagnacs.

GOUDOULIN

Veuve Goudoulin, Domaine de Bigor, Courrensan, 32330 Gondrin ***Tel: (62) 06 35 02***
XXX 3 · Réserve 5 · VSOP 8–10 · Hors d'Age · Vieil 16–20 · many single vintages

Madame Veuve Goudoulin began to sell the armagnacs from the family property, Domaine de Bigor in the Bas Armagnac, in 1934. In 1967 her grandson, Jacques Faure, took over the business side, while Christian Faure runs the property of 18 hectares planted with Ugni Blanc. They specialize in older, traditionally distilled armagnacs bought directly from the growers.

HAUT BARON

Cooperative de Cazaubon, 32150 Cazaubon
Tel: (62) 69 50 14
VSOP · Vintages: 1964, 1972

Very large cooperative with 451 members owning 751 hectares of vines, three-quarters Baco, the rest other hybrids. Classic stills. Owns stocks of 6,400 hectolitres of armagnacs dating back to 1923.

JANNEAU

50 Avenue d'Aquitaine, 32100 Condom
Tel: (62) 28 24 77
Tradition 4–5 · VSOP 10–12 · Napoléon 12–15 · XO 15–20 · Réserve 20–25 · Cinquentenaire 30–35 · 1961 · Domaine de Mouchac (BA) 1974

Visits: Monday to Friday 8.30 a.m.–12 noon and 2–6 p.m.

Founded by Pierre-Etienne Janneau in 1851. One of the oldest, biggest, most integrated and best firms in the region. Now has about one-eighth of the total market for armagnacs as well as major businesses in other local vinous products. In 1946, the founder's grandson, Etienne, died after running the firm since 1904. He was succeeded by his son Pierre, one of the rare graduates of the elite Ecole Polytechnique to work in the spirits business.

In 1976, needing financial and commercial reinforcement, he sold one-third of the firm to Martell. A further sale of 12% two years later still left the Janneaus with a majority. Janneau has over one-third of the armagnac market in Britain, while in France Janneau is sold through Martell's distribution company, headed by Pierre's son Michel. His brother Etienne stayed at home to run the firm.

Only 20,000 of the 150,000 hectolitres of wine which it bought in 1985–86 (75% Ugni Blanc; 15% Colombard; the rest, presumably Baco) went into the firm's stills. It has two sizeable continuous stills and three cognac-type stills, one of 100 hectolitres for the first *chauffe*, the other two, of 22 hectolitres each, for the *bonne chauffe*. It buys only limited quantities of old armagnacs. Most of Janneau's important stocks – 13,000 hectolitres of pure alcohol, equivalent to 4.7 million bottles – are housed in a fine 19th century cellar. All the young spirit has a spell in new oak. The armagnacs are preblended and steadily diluted during their maturation. The firm's stocks of old armagnac are large enough to ensure that the casks of older spirit are topped up by armagnac of the same vintage.

Janneau has a sensible policy for combining the two methods of distillation. The cheapest blend, Tradition, has 60% of quick-maturing, cognac-style spirit. It is light-orange, still rather fiery and estery on the nose. The VSOP, with 40% cognac-distilled spirit, is much longer and richer, with a fragrant nose.

The older armagnacs come exclusively from traditional stills. The XO, rich in colour, has a mature woody nose with a hint of the *rancio* to come. The Réserve has a deceptively light nose, but is long and elegant on the palate.

The firm also sells an interesting single-estate armagnac made from Ugni Blanc and Colombard grapes grown on a family property, the Domaine de Mouchac, in the Village du Frèche, the heart of the Bas Armagnac.

LABERDOLIVE
See Domaine d'Escoubes.

JEAN LADEVEZE
See La Boubée.

LEON LAFITTE
See Domaine de Boingnières.

LAMAZIERE
See St Vivant.

LAPEYROUZE
See St Vivant.

LARRESINGLE
Etablissements Papelorey SA, Rue des Carmes, 32100 Condom
Tel: (62) 28 15 33
XXX 3 · VSOP 8–10 · Napoléon 10 · Hors d'Age 18 · 20 Ans d'Age · 20
Comte de Lafitte (sold only in Japan)
One of the oldest firms in Armagnac, founded in 1837 by Hippolyte Papelorey, a native of Normandy who had married a Gascon girl. In 1896 their son Gabriel bought the magnificent Château de Larresingle, a walled village completed in 1250 (hence the claim on the labels that the firm was founded that year). Larresingle was the first firm to challenge Cognac by selling its product in bottle and not in cask.

The firm is now owned and run by Gabriel's grandson Maurice. It has no stills of its own and its cellars, in a former Carmelite convent in Condom, are even more remarkable than their contents. Larresingle uses armagnacs distilled both in the traditional and cognac fashion, which it buys new or up to 20 years old from growers in all three subregions. Two-thirds of its annual production of up to 800,000 bottles are sold outside France.

LAUDET
See Château de Laballe,
Parlebosc.

J. DE MALLIAC
Château de Malliac, 32250 Montreal-du-Gers
Tel: (62) 28 44 87
XXX 2–3 · VSOP 5–10 · Napoléon 5–12 · XO 6–15 · Hors d'Age 5–20+ · Hors d'Age Extra (BA) 5–20+ · Grand Bas Folle Blanche 47. (BA) 5% 20+ · Various single vintages
The de Mallac family, one of the most famous in the region, settled in Gascony in the 12th century. Parts of the château date from the Middle Ages. In the early 20th century the Bertholon family, which still controls de Malliac, established itself at the château and bought a well-known firm, Etablissments Comeille, founded in 1855.

The firm pioneered the term "Hors d'Age". More recently (and more usefully) it was the first to provide buyers with the date of bottling as well as of distillation. M. Bertholon has also escaped the domination of the styles imposed by the distillers, relying upon one only, Dr Garraud, whose work he closely supervises. M. Berthelon has also experimented with cognac-style distillation. After six to 12 months in new oak, to give them a "quick fix of tannin", the armagnacs are reduced to 50–55% and transferred to old oak. They are gradually reduced by stages of 3% at a time with distilled water. The result is a fine, elegant yet aromatic range of armagnacs, albeit still a bit fiery, up to the VSOP quality. The firm's best prize is a great rarity, an armagnac distilled exclusively from Folle Blanche grapes grown in the sandy soil of the far west of the Bas Armagnac. The vines have been producing since 1961, and since 1980 the firm has been selling a few thousand bottles. It is a rare treat with a deep nose, reminiscent of an oil distilled from flowers, a natural floral taste on the palate.

MARQUIS DE CAUSSADE
BP 38, Route de Cazaubon, 32800 Eauze
Tel: (62) 09 94 22
VSOP 11 · Napoléon: XO · 12 12+ · 21 21+ · Extra
Visits: 8.30 a.m.–5.30 p.m. throughout the year.
The most extraordinary story in Armagnac. Since the Middle Ages the Caussades have been one of the leading families in the region. In the 1930s Elliott de Caussade, who had settled near Condom, started to sell armagnacs under the family name. He took advantage of the maiden voyage of the *Normandie* in 1934 to transport the first bottle of armagnac ever seen in the USA (before Prohibition it had been imported in cask). Unfortunately he was killed in 1944 and the business was taken over by a friend, Gaston Baston, who also did a great deal to help create the BNIA. In 1964 the name was sold to the Bartissol group, and then bought up by the area's most ambitious cooperative, the Union de Cooperatives Viticoles de l'Armagnac, which brought together 6,000 growers accounting for 45% of the region's total production of white wines.

Overambition (and financial incompetence) proved a disastrous mixture and in 1980 the Credit Agricole moved in. This provided a major opportunity for Michel Coste, a former managing director of Otard, who was building up a group of small cognac merchants. He acquired 65% of a successor company for less than FF5 million. He bought the magnificent new premises and gained control of the biggest stock of old brandy in the region, with the added bonus of paying for it only as he sold it.

Since then Coste has exploited the stock of single-vintage armagnacs which he had inherited (especially the 1940 and the 1962); and has launched the first properly designed package for an armagnac, the new bottle for the Marquis de Caussade brand with a blue butterfly engraved on the bottle. Coste can rely on continuing supplies of traditionally distilled armagnacs from the former members of the UCVA. The Caussade brand itself is light, but full and aromatic.

MARQUIS DU LASSERRE

See Château de Lacaze.

MARQUIS DE LORNAC

See Marquis de Vibrac.

MARQUIS DE MONTESQUIEU

Route de Cazaubon, 32800 Eauze ***Tel: (62) 09 82 13.***
Exports: 120 Avenue du Maréchal Foch, 94015 Creteil ***Tel: (1 49) 81 50 15***
Monopole XXX 3+ · Napoléon 5+ · Soleil 10 · XO 10–15 · Vintages: 1942, 1959 and 1968 · Soleil 10 Danflou Vieil Armagnac · Trés Vieil Armagnac · Armagnac exceptionnel · Château d'Asterac (Cusenier)

Pierre de Montesquieu, Comte de Fezensac, a descendant of d'Artagnan, founded the firm in 1936 to sell the armagnacs produced on his own estates. In 1960 the business was taken over by the apéritif firm of Suze which also bought Vigneau, an old Cognac house with a superb stock of old armagnacs.

In 1965 the business was sold to Ricard, which also owns Cognac Bisquit (qv). It has maintained the firm's traditions and built it into one of the largest armagnac houses. It also produces armagnac for the well-known liquor firms of Danflou and (under the name of "Château d'Astarac") for Cusenier.

Half the firm's requirements come from its 90 hectare estate in the Bas Armagnac: 10 hectares are planted with Folle Blanche, the rest with Ugni Blanc. It also buys about 8,000 hectolitres of Ugni Blanc, two-thirds from the Bas-Armagnac, the remainder from the Ténarèze. All the wine is distilled in three classic armagnac stills to 53–55%. The firm buys only small lots of classically distilled armagnacs from individual distillers.

The firm's large cellars in Eauze, which it calls "the Cathedral", hold 3,500 casks. The brandy is left in new oak for six months, and is transferred to five year old casks for another two years before further maturing in old oak. The vintages are sold at their natural strength. Montesquieu is particularly proud of its prize-winning XO described by Gault and Millau as virile, which also has plenty of aroma from its careful production.

MARQUIS DE PUYSEGUR

See Chabot.

MARQUIS DE TERRAUBE
See André Daguin.

MARQUIS DE VIBRAC
Maison Henri Mounier, 7 Rue St Pierre, BP 134, 16104 Cognac ***Tel: (45) 82 03 39***
XXX 3–5 · VSOP 6–9 · Napoléon 10–15 · XO 15–20 · also Marquis de Lornac, largely sold in Belgium
Marquis de Vibrac is a subsidiary of a Cognac firm, Henri Mounier. It has no vines or stills of its own, but buys 40,000 hectolitres of distilled Ugni Blanc and Colombard from cooperatives.

MARQUIZA
See St Vivant.

MILLET
Francis Dèche, Millet, 32800 Eauze
Tel: (62) 09 87 91
Vintages: 1949–76
Family property for four generations. M. Dèche now has the wines from his 30 hectares of Colombard and Ugni Blanc vines distilled by Dargelos. He keeps the spirit in new oak from his own estate for up to two years.

DE MONTAL
Compagnie des Produits de Gascogne, 32000 Auch
Tel: (62) 08 81 81
VSOP 8 + · Réserve 12 + · Vintages: Cazaubon 1893–1943 · Panjas 1925–55 · Grand Bas Armagnac 1941 · Eauze 1960, 1961 · Ténarèze 1958, 1962
The de Montals have owned the Château de Rieutort for three centuries, but it has taken the brothers Olivier and Patrick to make the name famous throughout the world. They (and their armagnacs) have deservedly high reputations even in the USA, generally a desert so far as armagnac is concerned.

The de Montals are firm believers in blends, using stocks from a major cooperative for their basic brands. They also sell single-vintage armagnacs from various corners of Armagnac.

MONTROUGE
See Vignerons d'Armagnac.

LA MOTTE
M. Artigaux, La Motte, Cazeneuve, 32800 Eauze
Tel: (62) 09 90 27
Vintages: 1949, 1964, 1972–84
The wine from M. Artigaux's 30 hectares of Ugni Blanc is distilled to 55% and kept in old, local oak.

NISMES-DELCLOU
See Castarède.

PAPELOREY
See Larresingle.

PELLEHAUT
M. Gaston Béraut, 32250 Montreal-du-Gers
Tel: (62) 28 43 35
Vintages: 1974–83
For the past 12 years M. Béraut has been building his stock of armagnacs from his 120 hectare estate in the Ténarèze. He has them distilled (both ways) by Gimet and Mikalowski, and then keeps them in new oak for two years.

PLACHAT
Pierre Cornet, Plachat, Panjas, 32110 Nogaro
Tel: (62) 09 07 02
Vintages 1888–1974
M. Cornet is a famous distiller using both traditional and cognac-style stills. He has a superb collection of old armagnacs. It is the only estate in Panjas, to the east of the Bas Armagnac, which sells its own armagnacs. He distils the wine from his 14 hectares of Folle Blanche and Ugni Blanc himself, to 55–58% traditionally, 70–71% in the double stills. He does not use new oak, but houses new spirit in 40 hectolitre *tonneaux* of old wood. Otherwise casks are made from wood from his own estate.

PRINCE DE GASCOGNE
Diffusion des Produits Gascons, Rue d'Artagnan, 32440 Castelnau d'Auzan ***Tel: (62) 29 23 44***
XXX 2–3 · VSOP 5 · Napoléon 7 · Hors d'Age 10 · various vintages including 1945, 1956, 1964 · Rarissime (1934, still in cask)
Firm founded by a M. Etchard in 1899. Now half-owned by the family and half by a Madame Pagès. The firm is best known for its fruits bottled in armagnac. Besides bottling everyday fruits they also include exotica such as figs and kiwi fruit. The firm has a small estate of 5 hectares in the Ténarèze and buys 1,000 hectolitres of wine of all varieties which is distilled for it. Most of its requirements are supplied by individual growers, half from the Ténarèze, half from Bas Armagnac.

LE ROY DES ARMAGNACS
M. Gimet, Domaine Balenton Cazeneuve, 32800 Eauze ***Tel: (62) 09 90 01***
The most famous distiller in Armagnac with many original ideas. He also distils the armagnacs from the Baco and Ugni Blanc from his own 25 hectares of vines which he sells after keeping for one year in new oak.

SAINT VIVANT
Route de Nérac, 32100 Condom ***Tel: (62) 28 04 61***
VSOP 5 · XO 10. Also sold under names Baron de Gasconny, Carbonnel, Castaigne, Ducastaing, Lamazière, Lapeyrouze and Marquiza
The bottle carries the name of the 16th century Chevalier de Saint-Vivant, but the firm was founded only in 1947 by a M. Cogranne, allegedly the descendant of a Scottish immigrant called Cochran. It is now owned by the large drinks firm of La Martiniquaise, best-known in France for its down-market "scotch", Label 5.

LA SALLE PUISSANT
See La Boubée.

SAMALENS
32110 Laujuzan ***Tel: (62) 09 14 88***
XXX 3–5 · VSOP (BA) 7–10 · Napoléon 12–15 · Vieille Relique · Hors d'Age (BA) 15–20 · XO 20+
Visits: To 19th century cellars and the biggest distillery in Armagnac from 8.30 a.m.–12 noon and 2.30–6 p.m.
In 1882 Jean-François Samalens built a still and a cellar in his native village of Laujuzan. Basically, the family remained distillers and stockists until 1970. As a result it still has one of the biggest stocks of old armagnacs. Samalens' armagnacs are distributed by Rémy Martin, although the firm is still controlled by the brothers Jean and Georges Samalens, both well-known personalities on the armagnac scene.

Samalens own no vines but is otherwise well integrated. Of its eight stills four are cognac style each of 25 hectolitre capacity. The four continuous stills are centenarians, producing a mere trickle of rather heavy 55% armagnac, which is kept for six months in new oak ("de Gascogne" emphasize the Samalens) and then stored in old oak, either in a dry upper cellar or in the damper cellars below. The result is very typical of the Bas Armagnac, with some *rancio* even in the VSOP. Their Vieille Relique has all the nutty, pruny taste of the region.

SEIGNEUR DE LA TESTE
Cooperative de Condom, 32100 Condom
Tel: (62) 28 12 16
XXX · VSOP · Hors d'Age · Vintages 1943, 1951, 1960
Cooperative with 500 members owning 1,200 hectares. No indication of varieties grown. Two orthodox stills produce armagnac at 58 to 62%. Stocks of 3,500 hectolitres date back to 1943.

SEMPE
32290 Aignan ***Tel: 62.09.24.24*** **Paris office: 75 Rue St Lazare, 75009 Paris** ***Tel: (1 42) 85 33 66***
Fine 2 · VSOP · Napoléon 7–8 · Extra · Vieil 10 Armagnac · Imperial Réserve (in Baccarat crystal carafe). Vintages: 1934, 1942, 1955
Founded in 1934 by the 20 year-old Henri-Abel Sempé. Since then he has successfully combined business and politics, building up one of Armagnac's biggest firms while finding time to become the long-serving senator for the Gers. His two sons-in-law now work with him.

Sempé has only 20 hectares of its own vines in the Ténarèze, and a couple of modest-sized traditional stills. Most of its requirements come from the Colombard, Ugni Blanc and Piquepoult wines from small growers, distilled for the firm by a well-known specialist, Regert, at Villeneuve-de-Marsan. Four-fifths are distilled traditionally, the remainder *à la Charentaise*. The young brandies are stored for just less than two years in new oak. While the business was built up on cheaper, younger, unremarkable armagnacs, Sempé now offers some fine older brandies. The Fine (mostly sold in Belgium) is rather raw. But the Napoléon is rich and fine (even though it contains 30% Baco together with 50% Ugni Blanc and 20% Colombard). The Vieil is fine, deep, with a lot of rich *rancio*. The 1968 has a lighter nose, more floral with less *rancio* than the vieil, less woody than Sempé's other armagnacs.

LE TASTET

M. Cassous, Le Tastet Parlebosc, 40130 Gabarret
Tel: (58) 44 32 46
Vintages: 1977–84

One of the growers who has distilled his own grapes (from 40 hectares of young Folle Blanche, Colombard and Ugni Blanc vines) only since the 1970s. Like many recent entrants he is a firm traditionalist, distilling the wine to a mere 52% and keeping the new spirit in new oak for up to one year.

VERDUZAN

M. Morel, Cazeneuve, 32800 Eauze
Tel: (62) 29 10 92
Vintages: 1963, 1973

M. Morel has a substantial (60 hectare) estate in the Ténarèze, planted with classic varieties, distilled by Madame Dargelos. He does not use new oak for any of his 500 hectolitres of stock.

VEUVE GOUDOULIN

See Goudoulin.

VIGNERONS D'ARMAGNAC

Cooperative de Nogaro, 32110 Nogaro
Tel: (62) 09 01 79
XXX · VSOP · Napoléon. Also Castelfort and Montrouge brands.

Rather classy cooperative at Nogaro, a group of 400 growers owning 1,100 hectares, growing mostly Colombard and Ugni Blanc. Three orthodox stills; stocks of 9,000 hectolitres dating back to 1962.

OTHER FRENCH BRANDIES

In every wine-growing area of France thrifty peasants make marc from the pressings and lees, as well as a local "fine" from wine deemed unsuitable for drinking. None of these are thought of as more than local curiosities and, because the quantities are inevitably small, have never been widely marketed. The French government protects them, not through the more valuable *Appellation Contrôlée* system but only as *Eaux de Vie Règlementée* and has no real idea who makes them and how.

All the respondents to our questionnaire insisted that their brandies were merely by-products of their wine-making activities. Nevertheless, marc and fine are valued as a demonstration of the qualities of the original grapes.

ALSACE

The Alsatians have a long tradition of distilling their Gewürztraminer grapes – either by cooperatives, which return the spirit to the growers, or by a few independent distillers who generally also produce a wide range of eaux-de-vie from other fruits, selling the whole range both abroad and in France. As a result the – inevitably extremely aromatic – Marcs d'Alsace are better known than other local marcs produced only at an *artisanal* level.

BERTRAND

Distillerie Artisanale J. Bertrand, Uberback 67350 Pfaffenhoffen ***Tel: (88) 07 70 83***
Marc d'Alsace Gewürztraminer 45% · Vieux marc
The Bertrands have been distilling Alsace's fruits since 1874. They now use three "Holstein" type stills (pot-stills topped by a cylindrical rectifying chamber) and keep the marcs either in oak or in glass for up to three years.

GISSELBRECHT

Distillerie Artisanale, 6 rue Friedrich, 68150 Ribeauvillé ***Tel: (89) 73 64 36***
Eau-de-vie Reine-Claude d'Alsace · Marc de Tokay · Marc de Muscat · Marc de Riesling · Marc d'Alsace de Gewürztraminer. All 45%
Gisselbrecht is entitled to call itself *artisanal*. All its wide range of brandies (including its marcs) are double-distilled in two tiny (12 and 15 hectolitres respectively) Cognac-type stills. They are stored in glass containers under the roof of a warehouse, relying on the vagaries of the weather to provide character. Naturally they are lighter than marcs matured in wood.

LEHMANN

J & M Lehmann, Bischoffsheim, 67210 Obernai
Tel: (80) 22 31 20
Marc de Géwurztraminer 3

Another family firm, established in 1850, making a marc amongst a wide range of fruit brandies. Five stills, one inherited from the present owner's grandfather.

MASSENEZ
Distillerie G.E. Massenez, Dieffenbach au Val, 67220 Valle ***Tel: (88) 85 62 86***
Eau de Vie Elite des Fins Gourmets 2 · Eau de Vie Vieille Réserve 43% 4 · Eau de Vie Prestige 46% 7
One of Alsace's best-respected distillers with six modern stills. Massenez is particularly famous for its Framboise and Poire Williams, but also sells a range of marcs made from Gewürztraminer.

NUSSBAUMER
Distillerie Nussbaumer, 23 Grand Rue Steige, 67220 Ville ***Tel: (88) 57 16 53***
Marc d'Alsace Gewürztraminer
Only one of a very wide range of eau-de vie, mostly from other fruits, made by probably the largest independent distiller in Alsace.

BURGUNDY

There is a long Burgundian tradition of making marc (from what they locally call *gennes*) which are fermented in airtight vats for a month and then distilled, traditionally by travelling distillers. These produce spirits of a mere 52% with the same potential intensity and grapiness as the rather similar stills used in Armagnac. In theory marc *egrappé* made from a raw material without stalks should be smoother, but today most bunches are destalked anyway so that all marc is, effectively, *egrappé*. The "fine" should, in theory, be made from wine; in fact, it is also made from the lees.

Today most of the "leftovers" in Burgundy are distilled by two industrial establishments, Vedrenne at Nuits-St-Georges, and the Distillerie de Bourgogne at Beaune. Only a handful of others have their own stills and there are few ambulant distillers left. This is unfortunate for, at its best a Marc de Bourgogne, aged 10 years in the oak casks used for wine, can provide a rich, oily, grapey intensity unmatched by any other distilled spirit. They remain relatively unappreciated, partly because they are generally drunk at the end of stupendous Burgundian meals, and partly because they are so strong (often sold at 45% to 50%).

ALLEXANT
Domaine Jean Allexant, Saint Marie la Blanche, 21200 Beaune ***Tel: (80) 26 60 77***
Marc de Bourgogne 6 · Fine de Bourgogne 6
Sixteen hectare holding with its own Burgundy-style still, a mere 10 years old.

JULES BELIN
3 Rue des Seuillets, BP 43, 21702 Nuits-St-Georges ***Tel: (80) 61 07 74***
Marc Vieux à la Cloche Egrappé 10 - 20 · Marc 24 Ans d'Age 24+

The firm has been maturing and selling eaux-de-vie since 1817 and M. Claude Lanvin maintains the tradition.

BOUCHARD

Bouchard Père & Fils, Au Château, BP 70, 21202 Beaune ***Tel: (80) 22 14 41***
Fine Bourgogne 41.5% 5 · Marc de Bourgogne des Domaines du Château de Beaune 41.5% 5
One of Burgundy's biggest merchants offers marc made from the lees of its own extensive estates.

CAVES DE HAUTES COTES

Route de Pommard, 21200 Beaune
Tel: (80) 24 63 12
Fine Bourgogne 45% 75cl · Marc de Bourgogne 45% 75cl
A large cooperative whose 157 members have 360 hectares of vines. They distil locally in venerable stills. The spirits are then matured in new oak. The marc received a gold medal at the 1987 Paris Concours Agricole – a notable honour.

CHATEAU DE MEURSAULT

Comte de Moucheron, Meursault
Marc du Château 41% 10
Classic Burgundian marc, half Pinot, half Chardonnay.

CHATEAU DE POMMARD

Jean-Louis Laplanche, Château de Pommard, 21630 Pommard ***Tel: (80) 22 07 99***
Marc du Château de Pommard
M. Laplanche has the marc from his Pinot Noir distilled by a travelling distiller and then ages it for at least 15 years in new Burgundian *pièces* of 228 litres. He sells the brandy to private customers in France and abroad.

CORTON GRANCEY

Louis Latour, 18 rue des Tonnelliers, 21200 Beaune ***Tel (80) 22 31 20***
Marc de Corton-Grancey 8
This is a superb marc which is rich and fruity. The dry marc is stored in sealed wooden vats for six months before distillation. The new spirit (a mere 50%) is then matured in new oak.

DOMAINES DU CHATEAU DE BEAUNE

See Bouchard

DOMAINE BERNARD DELAGRANGE

21190 Meursault ***Tel: (80) 21 22 72***
Vieux Marc de Bourgogne 44% 8 · Vieille Fine de Bourgogne 44% 9
M. Delagrange regrets the steady disappearance of the custom of growers distilling their lees and marcs, sending them instead to Beaune for industrial distillation. He has the lees and marcs from his 22 hectare property (owned by his family for generations) distilled by a travelling distiller and ages them for eight years in Burgundy oak casks.

DOMAINE DES HAUTES CORNIERES

Philippe Chapelle et Fils, Domaine des Hautes-Cornières, 21590 Santenay ***Tel: (80) 20 60 09***

Marc de Bourgogne 41% 75 cl · Marc de Bourgogne 1964 · Fine de Bourgogne 40% 73 cl

The Chapelles aim for a "very supple" style in their marcs, which are aged from five to 10 years.

DOMAINE DUJAC

Morey Saint Denis, 21220 Gevrey Chambertin
Tel: (80) 34 32 58

Marc de Bourgogne 1970 41% 75 cl

Jacques Seysses, the owner, has always loved good marc. Finding it exceedingly difficult to buy, he began by having his marc distilled in 1969, the year after he began making wine at the domaine. However, he did not start selling until 1983, when his superb, classic marc, strongly stamped with the oiliness of the grape pips – one of the few vintage marcs – had been aged in new wood for 14 years.

DOMAINE PRIEUR BRUNET

21590 Santenay ***Tel: (80) 20 60 56***

Marc de Bourgogne · Fine Bourgogne

The domaine has its own 80-year-old still, and the new marcs are lodged in oak for 10 years.

DOMAINE DE LA ROMANEE CONTI

Vosne-Romanée, 21700 Nuits St Georges
Tel: (80) 61 04 57

Marc de Bourgogne du Domaine de la Romanée-Conti · Fine Bourgogne du Domaine de la Romanée-Conti

The finest of all Burgundian estates offers a distinguished, well matured brandy, but in limited quantities.

JOSEPH DROUHIN

7 Rue d'Enfer, BP 29, 21201 Beaune
Tel: (80) 24 68 88

Marc de Bourgogne 8-10 · Fine de Bourgogne 8-10

One of the most respected of all Burgundy merchants. Believes that his marc and fine contribute to the image of his name, so they must be good.

LIGNIER

Georges Lignier et fils, Morey-Saint Denis, 21220 Gevrey-Chambertin ***Tel: (80) 34 32 55***

Vieux Marc de Bourgogne 7

A highly reputable grower who naturally takes some care over his prize-winning marc, which is truly *égrappé*, and kept for at least seven years in new Burgundy casks.

MOMMESSIN

La Grange St Pierre, 71850 Charnay Les Macon
Tel: (85) 34 47 74

Marc du Clos de Tart 5+ · Fine du Clos de Tart 5+ · Marc de Bourgogne

Well-known Burgundy merchant which buys in its eaux-de-vie. Particularly proud of its prize-winning fine.

GUY ROULOT

1 Rue Charles Giraud, 21190 Meursault
Tel: (80) 21 21 65
Marc de Bourgogne 43% 8+ · Fine Bourgogne 43% 8+
The Roulot family has been distilling for its neighbours since 1860 and until 1983 went round the district with a mobile still. Since then M. Roulot has produced marc for himself and his customers. He takes great care with his old still, eliminating heads and (if below quality) tails as well.

THIBAUT

Jacques Thibaut, Vaux les Grenard, 21540 Somzernon ***Tel: (80) 39 46 35***
Eau de Vie de Marc · Eau de Vie de Fine
Professional distiller with two stills, one with steam, the other similar to the *en calandre* system used in Champagne.

CHAMPAGNE

FINE DE CHAMPAGNE, MARC DE CHAMPAGNE

Jean Goyard et Cie, 51160 Ay ***Tel: (26) 50 10 43***
In the past many Champagne firms distilled their own marcs and fines, but now they are all distilled by the family firm of Goyard which takes all the lees from the region – the quantity is so great that M. Keene, grandson of the founder, can select the better lees before using the rest to make industrial alcohol. He produces delicate and aromatic brandies because marc made from grapes which have been pressed whole, as is the case when making champagne, contains a lot of sugar and no alcohol. By contrast the marc used in Burgundy comes from vats where the raw material has already been destalked and fermented. The fine is made mostly from the wine rich in sediment which pops out of the champagne bottle when it is disgorged. M. Keene likes these: "wines from noble grape varieties which start with yeasts, lots of lees and are stuffed full of aromatics".

Both marc and fine are distilled *en calandre*. The wines are first heated by steam in three interconnected vessels each holding about 400 litres. The fumes, at about 20% alcohol, are then distilled to about 70%. Some of the marcs are sold to makers of "grape brandy" to provide flavour.

COTES-DU-RHONE

CHATEAU GRILLET

Neyret-Gachet, Château Grillet, Verin, 42410 Pelussin
Eau de Vie de Marc de Château Grillet
This famous estate makes a tiny quantity of marc.

PINCHON

MM Pinchon & Niero, 20 Rue des Granges, 69420 Condrieu ***Tel: (74) 59 50 22***
Marc de Condrieu Cépage Viognier 45%
A small family estate, making one of the rare marcs from the precious Viognier grape. Stored for three years in stainless steel, the marc retains the fruity aroma of the original grape.

VIDAL-FLEURY

BP 12, 69420 Ampuis ***Tel: (74) 56 10 18***

Vieux Marc de Côte Rôtie 43% 12-15

One of the very few marcs made on the Côte Rôtie, using the local Syrah and Viognier grapes grown on M. Guigal's 10 hectare estate.

JURA

There is a long tradition in the Jura of making marc and eau-de-vie, now entitled to the appellation Eau de Vie de Franche-Comté.

JEAN BOURDY

Caves Jean Bourdy, Arlay, 39140 Bletterans
Tel: (84) 85 03 70

Marc de Franche-Comté 6 50%

M. Bourdy's family has long distilled its marc and for the past 20 years Christian Bourdy has headed a local group of distillers. He himself has three small continuous stills and ages his marc in small wooden casks for six or seven years, after which, he says, they have an aroma of "enpirum".

CHATEAU D'ARLAY

Arlay, 39140 Bletterans ***Tel: (84) 85 04 22***

Vieux Marc de Franche-Comté 50% · Vieille Fine de Franche-Comté Comte René de Laguiche 50%

This historic château was once the property of the Nassau family which still occupies the throne of Holland – the present Queen of the Netherlands has Comtesse d'Arlay as one of her titles. The vineyards are, reputedly, the oldest in the Jura – their wines are still served at the French presidential palace. Comte René de Laguiche, the present owner, opens the château to visitors in the summer and makes a range of wines and spirits. The marc and the fine are both aged in oak for between five and 10 years.

HUBERT CLAVELIN

Le Vernois, 39210 Voiteur, Jura ***Tel: (84) 25 31 58***

Eau de Vie de Marc de Franche-Comté 50% 4 · Vieux Marc du Jura 50% 6

M. Clavelin distils the marc from the Chardonnay on his 23 hectare estate in his own small still.

HENRI MAIRE

Château Montfort, 39600 Arbois ***Tel: (84) 66 12 34***

Marc Egrappé 50% 6 · Vieux Marc Egrappé 50% 10 · Marc Flambé 50%

The "King of the Jura", who sells three in every five bottles of wine from the region, naturally owns his own stills. He double distils his marcs and matures them in oak.

PUPILLON

Cooperative Fruitière Vinicole de Pupillon, 39600
Tel: (84) 66 12 88

Marc du Jura 48% 3 · Fine 48% 3

A village cooperative near Arbois which makes a wide range of wines. It hires a travelling distiller.

PROVENCE

BUNAN

Pierre & Paul Bunan, 83740 La Cadière d'Azur
Tel: (94) 98 72 76
Marc de Muscat de Bandol 50% 1 · Marc de Bandol Egrappé 50% 5 · Vieux Marc de Bandol Egrappé 50% 7 – all three sold under two brand names, Mas de La Rivière and Moulin des Costes.

The Bunans are the proud possessors of the oldest still in the region. It is a single-pass, cognac-type alembic, still heated by coal, made in Marseilles and brought to Bandol in 1920. For 50 years it was tended lovingly by one of the few female distillers in France, Madame Josephine Boetti. She bequeathed it to the Bunans and found a worthy disciple in young Laurent Bunan, a qualified oenologist.

CHATEAU DE PIBARNON

Comte de St Victor, Château de Pibarnon, 83740 La Cadière d'Azur ***Tel: (94) 90 12 73***
Vieux Marc de Bandol 1978

Luckily for lovers of aromatic marc, the Comte de St Victor adores armagnac as much as the prize-winning wines he makes on his 35 hectare estate. His enthusiasm led him to buy an ancient armagnac still which he uses exclusively to distil the marc from his Mourvèdre grapes, taking care to discard the heads and tails. The marc is matured for at least eight years in new oak casks, bought from a cooper in Burgundy, and the brandies sold without additives. The result, he says, is "a lovely aroma of plums, prunes and nuts, the unmistakable sign of a great armagnac". Such enthusiasm is welcome and could be infectious.

COMMANDERIE DE LA BARGEMONE

13760 Saint Cannat ***Tel: (42) 28 22 44***
Paris office: 34 Avenue de Messine, 75008 Paris
Tel: (1 45) 63 06 20
Marc des Coteaux d'Aix en Provence

M. J.P. Rozan has a 70 hectare estate near Aix en Provence, planted with some impressive varieties (including Cabernet). His marc is distilled for him by a travelling distiller and aged for seven years in tiny (120 litres) oak casks.

JOSEPH MERLIN

Domaine de Suriane, 13250 Saint Chamas
Tel: (91) 93 91 91
Eau de Vie de Marc Originaire de Provence 54% and 61% 6-8

M. Merlin has been selling marc from his 38.5 hectare estate for 40 years, so has had plenty of time to perfect his style. He has his marc distilled for him, but matures it himself in old cognac casks which, he says, gives it a much-appreciated taste of cognac.

SPAIN

The History of Spanish Brandy

To the Anglo-Saxons, Spanish brandy is automatically associated with sweetness and stickiness. This profoundly biased view springs from an inherited belief that all grape spirits not made in France are unimportant, somehow impure and second-rate. Spanish brandy makers present a challenge to both these errors.

More brandy is produced in Spain than in France – or indeed than in any other European country. During the decade 1975–85 Spanish brandy makers sold an average of 162 million bottles at home and 21.7 million abroad. Moreover, the basic quality is surprisingly high – partly because Spain is one of the few European countries where "brandy" refers only to spirit distilled exclusively from grapes, and containing no neutral spirit. The average level of quality is being maintained and improved because the business is concentrated in the hands of a dozen or so firms, mostly sherry producers. They are in a strong position to promote their wares throughout the world and are obviously interested in preserving their reputation for quality whether they are selling brandy or sherry – the producers of Jerez brandy account for 92% of the home market and 96% of exports. Over the past half century Spanish brandies have dominated the Latin American markets. More recently they have challenged the French hegemony in other markets, notably in Germany and Italy. Their quality is such that they can hope to make their presence felt in any country not obsessed by the generally more austere spirits offered by the French.

Spanish brandies vary enormously, not just in quality, but in style, and the ways they are made. The first distinction is between the majority, produced by the sherry firms, and two brands made in Catalonia by Torres and Mascaró. These are among the most interesting of Spanish brandies but, as can be seen from their entries in the directory which follows, the French influence is predominant. They are made in cognac-type stills from undrinkably acid wines, whereas the Jerezanos have always believed that the base wine should be drinkable and not overly acid. In Jerez they have fashioned their own styles and these, while all quite distinct from the French, vary wildly.

Apart from the two Catalan producers, Spanish brandy is almost invariably warmer, richer, fuller and, in many cases, deliberately sweeter than anything produced in France. "According to the experts," wrote Manoel Gonzalez y Gilbey, "the three rules for good brandy are that it should be fiery on the tongue, velvety on the throat, and warm on the stomach."* By obeying such rules it cannot offer the subtleties of an old cognac or armagnac but it can offer a much higher degree of reliability than most French brandies, together with – and Gonzalez' experts were being unfair to their own country's products – an unmistakable velvetiness of its own, on the palate as on the nose.

*In his invaluable chapter on Brandy in *Sherry: the Noble Wine*

The Arab Tradition

Spanish brandy is older – and younger – than any French spirit. The Spanish, especially those in the south, learnt a great deal from the Arabs, who brought civilization to the country which they occupied for several centuries. Jerez, in the south, was reconquered by the Christians in the 13th century, and it was for a long time the frontier with Arab Spain (hence the name Jerez de la Frontera), yet Moorish influence penetrated political boundaries. Among the lessons learnt by the Christians was the art of alcohol distillation – the Spanish use the Arab words alcohol and alembic: but they have also retained the Arab-derived term "alquitara" for a pot-still.

In Spain the origins of distillation are generally associated with a celebrated late 13th century Spanish doctor, Arnaldo de Vilanova. "But it is impossible to say," writes Manoel Gonzalez, "whether Vilanova was the initiator and passed his knowledge to the Arabs or vice versa." Vilanova is also claimed as a native by the brandy makers of Catalonia, who were already writing about *esperit de vin* – the name of the Appellation established for Catalan brandies in 1985.

By the late 16th century distillation was profitable enough for the Jesuits to be granted the proceeds from an excise tax on spirits to help them found a college in Jerez. In the following two centuries a particular type of spirit became known as "holandas". Originally the spirit was probably imported – from Holland, as the name indicates – to fortify the wines of Jerez before they were exported as sherry. By the mid-19th century the Jerezanos were producing their own spirit, mainly from the *vin-de-presse*, the last squeezings from the grapes used for sherry, and exporting it, as holandas, to Holland. It was distilled to a mere 65–70% and was thus different from the raw, higher-strength spirits known then as now as "aguardiente" or "destillados."

The First Commercial Brandies

In the last quarter of the 19th century Spanish brandy ceased to be a mere raw material, an additive, and was transformed into a saleable product. Myth has it that Pedro Domecq Lustau, a member of the distinguished family of sherry shippers, could not find a buyer for a couple of casks of sherry, forgot about them for several years, and was then so struck by their bouquet and flavour that he decided to redistil the contents as brandy. Thus, allegedly, was born Fundador, the pioneering Spanish brandy, which was first marketed in 1874 and is still synonymous with Spanish brandy in many Anglo-Saxon markets.

Domecq's timing was perfect. The year before he sold his first bottle phylloxera struck the Charente. By the late 1870s the supply of real cognac was starting to dry up. Buyers (and the less scrupulous Cognac houses) began a frantic search for replacements from vineyards not yet plagued by the louse. Since phylloxera did not reach Jerez until the early 1890s, Jerez brandy enjoyed an inevitably brief boom.

The pseudo-cognac trade was pioneered by Francisco Ivison O'Neale, a noted figure in the sherry trade who deliberately and craftily used a vague brand name, La Marque Spéciale, which omitted both his name and the geographical origin of the spirit. Naturally, all the other sherry houses followed his lead. The famous firm of Terry, for instance, started to distil brandies which it described as made "from the best wines of Jerez" as soon as it was founded in 1883. By 1908 the word "coñac" had been approved for inclusion in the Spanish dictionary. It remained the habitual name for brandy in Spain until the country's entry into the European Economic Community in 1985 forced the Spaniards to (officially) abandon the name.

During the boom numerous cognac-type stills were built, often to French designs, although some I saw at Gonzalez Byass had been adapted so that the wine was heated once only. The brandy was then matured in soleras, the system used for maturing sherry. The mature brandy is drawn from the lowest row of a bank of casks. These are then replenished from above, with new spirit being poured into the topmost casks. As with sherry, the soleras can be over a century old. At Gonzalez Byass I tasted a brandy from a solera begun with the 1886 vintage. It was a splendid deep chestnut brown colour, with a touch of red and a lovely warm nose but, unsurprisingly, tasted bitter, of pure tannic wood.

The burst of prosperity was inevitably temporary. Jerez was hit by phylloxera while Cognac started to replant with grafted vines. However, a residual business remained. In the 1930s Manoel Gonzalez emphasized that local brandy had: "a virtual monopoly of the home market and is also much appreciated in other countries". The trade had grown up and the production process greatly improved. According to Gonzalez:

> *Some of the Holandas used in Jerez itself and pure wine alcohol is also produced in small quantities, but as alcohol is a neutral product used principally for the fortification of wines it is generally brought in from other districts of Spain (principally Ciudad Real and La Mancha) where wine can be obtained more cheaply than in Jerez, Sherry being naturally considerably more expensive than ordinary table wines.*

The wine no longer came from Jerez, but from less noble vineyards; a variety of spirit, some relatively pure, some more characterful, was being made — but on a small scale.

Then another disaster, this time man-made, intervened to help the Spanish brandy business. For three years from 1936 to 1939 the Spanish Civil War created a demand for brandy to keep up the spirits of the troops on both sides. In the misery of the 20 years after the civil war an increasing flood of cheap brandies, not only from Jerez, but also from Murcia and northern Spain, provided the kind of raw energy historically required by manual workers in cold climates – winters in Spain can be very cold, and miserably rainy as well. Production in Jerez more than doubled between the mid-1940s and 1960 as Spanish workers became used to taking a cafe-coñac on their way to work in the mornings (in the Basque country one has only to ask for a *completo* and one gets coffee, brandy and a cigar). But the real take off was in the 1960s. By 1970 the Spaniards were drinking 140 million bottles of brandy a year, $3\frac{1}{2}$ bottles per head, a far higher rate than any other country in the world (Hong Kong excepted).

The Jerez Firms

Most of the benefit went to a handful of firms in Jerez. Ironically, the marketing experts from the international groups, which controlled so many sherry shippers, completely ignored the business; they were too obsessed with the idea that cognac was the only marketable spirit. So the field was left open to a handful of native concerns, especially Domecq, Osborne, Bobadilla, Terry and Gonzalez Byass which, then as now, dominate the Spanish brandy scene. It was only their profits from brandy which enabled some of them to remain independent during the bad years of the late 1970s when the megalomaniac Ruiz Mateos was forcing the price (and quality) of sherry down in a seemingly unstoppable spiral. Ironically, had he paid more attention to brandy, he might have kept afloat – although he did acquire one important brandy producer, the family firm of Terry, using the stocks of brandy acquired with the other firms he had bought to introduce a new brand, Gran Duque d'Alba (*see* Bodegas Internacionales).

The result is that today the trade is firmly under the control of the handful of firms listed on pages 119–127. By EEC regulations these firms can no longer use the magic name coñac and know they face competition from French cognacs which at the moment are uncommercially expensive within Spain.

In the home market their biggest worry is not foreign competition but a steady erosion of the market as a whole. As with so many other spirits associated with a particular generation, a particular stage in the social and economic development of a country, sales of brandies within Spain have stagnated over the past decade as work has become less hard, the workers requiring less raw energy (and less need to counter the misery of their lot).

As the table on page 119 reveals, this stagnation has been hidden by wild fluctuations as taxes have increased by a series of shocks which, however, were not too sudden to prevent buyers from stocking up in anticipation. These shocks have lifted the duty from a mere 20 pesetas a litre in 1970 to 550 pesetas in 1986 – with more to come when Spain eventually gets round to following the EEC's rules about equalization of excise duties. Brandies also pay VAT, as also ever-increasing luxury and welfare taxes, so that today just over half the sale price of a bottle of cheap brandy is tax.

The Spanish Taste

Within Spain the trade has shifted. The brandies are mostly less sweet than they were in the 1930s when Gonzalez noted that outside Spain: "many markets prefer their brandies less sweet than the Spanish domestic customer". Social customs have also changed. Brandy used to be predominantly drunk in bars but in the last 10 years there has been a gradual increase in the take-home trade, which represented 47% of sales in 1975, 10% more than in 1965. This shift has favoured companies, like Osborne and Gonzalez Byass, which have strong sales forces marketing a whole range of their products to grocers and, increasingly, to supermarket chains. It has notably damaged Domecq, formerly the market leader in the cheaper brands, which still retains just over three-quarters of total sales. Its commercial policies were disastrous enough to permit Terry's Centenario, Osborne's Veterano, and, above all, Gonzalez Byass's Soberano, to dominate the sector. Soberano now has nearly a quarter of the market for cheaper brandies: the top three account for nearly three-fifths of the total; Bobadilla's 103 White Label has nearly one-tenth, while including Fundador, Garvey's Esplendido and Agustin Blasquez's Felipe II, the top seven have 90% of the market.

The trade (now followed by the legislation) fits other brandies into two superior brackets, Reserva and Gran Reserva, and is naturally trying to compensate for decreasing sales of cheaper brandies by concentrating upon these better brandies. The Reservas account for over two million cases, one-fifth of the total (and more than twice the total production of armagnac). The sector is dominated by Osborne's highly profitable Magno, while Gonzalez' Lepanto – a completely different style of brandy – is the best-selling Gran Reserva, though all Gran Reservas only add up to a mere 100,000 cases. All three sectors are dominated by a handful of brands, largely from the same firms – although Sánchez Romate's Cardenal Mendoza is held to be the most desirable brandy of them all.

Exports

The brandy firms are compensating for stagnant sales at home by trying to spread the gospel of Spanish brandy throughout the world. This is not a new development. As early as the 1930s, Gonzalez noted that brandy could only be exported to those countries: "where import duties have not made the price prohibitive". This is an eternal refrain for a product whose natural markets are in Latin America. A number of firms, especially Domecq, now distil brandies there, or import the concentrated brandy from Spain and dilute it on the spot. For some years Domecq relied for the bulk of its profits upon its Mexican subsidiary, which still produces over four million cases of its Presidente brandy a year, making it by far the world's biggest selling grape brandy.

Other firms have set up more-or-less profitable local distilleries in countries as far apart as Venezuela, Brazil, Colombia and Argentina where, 15 years ago, Terry was producing 250,000 cases. Today these markets are mostly closed to official imports. The only way round is to smuggle (a major business runs across the Rio Grande from Texas into Mexico) or import concentrated brandy which is diluted and bottled locally.

In the long term the Spaniards have great hopes of the drinkers in Germany and Italy, both large markets for brandy, and both, by no coincidence, countries free from Anglo-Saxon preconceptions. In the past shippers were hampered because they had to spend precious foreign currency to introduce and promote their products, a very expensive experience.

Probably the Spaniards' biggest problem is to escape from the confines of the ethnic market, although these can be substantial. Rich Cubans in Miami, for instance, are doughty quaffers of the better Spanish brandies, while in

Germany Spanish brandy, originally introduced by the millions of Spanish *gastarbeiter*, has now been found very much to the taste of native German drinkers.

MAKING THE BRANDY

More than 90% of Spanish brandy is sold by the sherry firms of Jerez. Their brandies differ greatly from those of the only two other firms making Spanish brandy – Torres and Mascaro – whose distinctive styles are described under their entries in the Directory. The following description applies only to Jerez brandies.

Originally, brandy was made from grapes grown around Jerez; now it is only matured there. Almost invariably it is made from the rather characterless Airén grapes grown and fermented in La Mancha, the vast, bleak upland plateau a hundred miles south of Madrid. It is then distilled in Tomelloso, a dusty, sprawling town in the heart of the vineyard. According to Jancis Robinson the Airén is the most-planted vine in the world because of the requirements of the Spanish brandy industry. But La Mancha is arid; under Spanish law no irrigation is allowed, so the vines are planted very sparsely, at 1,200 to 1,600 to the hectare. The yield is also low at 25–28 hectolitres per hectare. So the Jerezianos need nearly half a million hectares of vines to satisfy their requirements.

Although the harvest starts at the end of August the wine, at 12 to 14% alcohol, is stronger, less acid, than the raw material used to produce cognac or armagnac (thus the aromas it contains are multiplied less in the distillation than in France). At 70% the Airén has been concentrated a mere five times. The Ugni Blanc of Cognac, harvested at between 8% and 9%, is concentrated up to eight times. Moreover, because of the vast quantities involved, distillation in La Mancha does not stop in the spring, but can continue well into the hot Spanish spring and summer. The later the wine is distilled, the less acid it becomes and the greater the need for the addition of sulphur dioxide. Fortunately the sulphur can be dissipated through distillation but the residual sulphur does cause a certain coarseness in the throat.

Nevertheless the sheer concentration of the Spanish brandy business has helped to maintain minimum qualities. None of the firms grows any grapes in La Mancha, buying the wine from the enormous cooperative wineries (one of which presses up to 100 million kilos of grapes a year), merely ensuring minimum quality standards. Distillation is another matter. Because they all have their own special requirements, many of the firms have either set up their own stills or (like Osborne) bought up a distiller some years ago. If they do have to buy in the newly distilled spirit they ensure that the distillers maintain strict standards. Domecq, which in the past set the pace for the industry, is particularly insistent upon the elimination of butanol and ethyl butyrate which give the brandy nasty overtones of cheesy feet.

The Methods

The peculiarity of Spanish brandy is that it can be distilled in any one of four ways: continuously, either to very high

proof or to cognac-style strength and, if Cognac-type pot stills are used, then the spirit can be distilled once or twice. The language used does not help to define the styles with any clarity. The Spanish word *aguardiente* (eau-de-vie), covers anything below rectified spirit; only a handful of technicians in each house seem to know the precise mix of spirits used in their brands. At the moment the Spanish regulations merely divide newly distilled grape spirit into three types:
Holandas - Baja Graduaçion – below 70%
Aguardientes - Medra Graduaçion – 70–80%
Destilados de Vino - Alta Graduaçion – 80–95%

The EEC Regulations
Since the new EEC regulations require newly distilled spirit to be a maximum of 86%, in future there will only be two types: Holandas and Destilados de Alta Graduacion. But even today's destillado, at 95%, still retains some of the fruity qualities of the original grape and is by no means a neutral spirit. Newly distilled destillado has a rather medicinal feel about it (because of the ethyl acetate) but is recognizably distilled wine. The vinous qualities will be even more strongly recognizable when the maximum strength of the newly distilled brandies is reduced to 86%. This reduction will have a major effect on the quality of the cheaper Spanish brandies, which consist very largely, or entirely, of destillado, and whose character is more or less determined by ageing and additives. In the future they should be more naturally grapey, requiring fewer additives.

The continuous stills used for destillados have up to 60 plates to rectify the spirit. This is treble the number used to produce holandas, the unique spirit which is the basis of most middle-range Spanish brandy. Nowhere else in the world do distillers produce a continuously distilled spirit of such low strength and hence such grapiness. Yet holandas is not a deliberate choice to suit a particular Spanish style, but rather the result of an historical accident. The Spaniards acquired the habit of distillation to 65–70% – albeit in cognac-type stills – to supply the Dutch, and kept to that same strength even when they changed over to continuous distillation. The fruitiness of the newly distilled holandas can be increased if, like Domecq, one uses a fine spray of hot water to attack the *vinasses*, the mass of lees at the bottom of the still. This hydroselection increases the concentration of esters. Any newly distilled holandas is surprisingly rich and oily, and promises what might be described as "congeneric" richness.

Nevertheless, for their best brandies the Jerezianos stick to modified pot-stills, making what they call "alquitara". They almost invariably use separate rectifying chambers to distil directly to the required 65–70% using the word alquitara indiscriminately both for single and double-distilled spirit. It is, of course, much more expensive than continuous distillation, adding between five and eight pesetas to the cost of every litre of spirit.

Again it is history, reinforced by their experience with the rich wines of Jerez and the ripe, if characterless, grapes grown in La Mancha, which explains why they distil only once. According to Manoel Gonzalez: "Certain wines of less bouquet give better results when distilled only once, and the spirit obtained has a nicer bouquet: this is the case with almost all wines except the special ones made in the Charente." Gonzalez describes how "rectifying discs were placed near the outlet of the boiler; these are refrigerated externally by running water, the flow of which can be increased, reduced or suppressed at will." One can still see the three discs above the (unused) century-old cognac-type stills in the Gonzalez bodegas today.

The stills used to produce alquitara are much the same size as those in Cognac, holding about 25 hectolitres of wine, but the Jerezianos still use external wood heating, long since abandoned in Cognac (the wood needs transporting some distance since the uplands of La Mancha are almost bereft of trees). They admit that distilling once in a pot-still, relying on a separate rectifying chamber, or rectifying discs, to increase the strength, inevitably involves a reduction in the potential fruitiness of the brandy compared with cognac. Nevertheless even single-distilled pot-still brandy is superior to that produced continuously – especially if, like Domecq or Bobadilla, one distils it exclusively in the winter and can thus use minimal quantities of sulphur dioxide. As in Cognac the copper from which the still is constructed acts as a catalyst to produce fruity esters, and the resulting spirit resembles a newly distilled cognac, raw and oily like grappa. Its delicate, almost tea-like, nose provides a promise of excitements to come. If, again like Domecq, the wine is distilled on its lees, the result is potentially even richer and more concentrated.

The Solera System

Newly distilled Spanish brandy is inevitably less characterful than new cognac or armagnac. The grapes are not as acid, the wine-making is routine (and involves some sulphur), and the distillation methods preserve less of the original grapiness. The key to Spanish brandies, whatever the style, lies in the wood and additives used, and that most are lodged entirely in soleras, banks of 500 litre oak casks, previously used to mature sherry. With brandy, as with sherry, the spirit is moved down the casks, with new spirit going in at the top as the final product is drawn off from the bottom rank of casks. In Gonzalez' day, the better brandies were matured for a time in small oak casks before being reduced (to 44%), sweetened with a little sugar syrup, and then transferred to the solera for faster maturation. Today most brandies spend their whole maturation period in the soleras. This makes the maturation dramatically different to all other brandies.

The first difference is the sheer speed of the ageing. The Jerezanos contrast "dynamic" ageing in soleras with the "static" ageing found in Cognac. The final quality can be altered according to the frequency with which the spirit is transferred between casks – often three or four times a year. But however infrequently the spirit is moved through the system, dynamic ageing speeds up the maturation process considerably. A year-old holandas is already developing into a drinkable produce while a two-year old alquitara from a solera is as mature as a three or four year old cognac.

Crucially, too, with brandy, as with sherry, the solera system almost guarantees a consistent style.

The Choice of Oak

Another difference with fine French brandies is in the oak. The Jerezanos now use exclusively American white oak (although until recently a lot of the brandy was lodged in Portugese oak, because they could not afford new American oak for their sherries). Even when new it has only one-third of the tannin of French oak. Nevertheless, the final style is set principally by the nature of the original brandy – adding, say, one-fifth of destillados reduces the maturation time compared with using pure holandas – combined with the length of time it spends in the system. Other factors also intervene: casks formerly used for olorosos obviously give a different character to the brandy than those formerly used for fino (Sánchez Romate's Cardenal Mendoza is the obvious example of an "oloroso-style" brandy).

Chemically in a static system there is a stratum of large molecules near the wood because the smaller molecules of water leak through the wood. When the brandy is moved, thereby exposing it to the air, the molecules are churned up and multiply the aldehydes. The same effect is created by the use of sulphur dioxide in wine and the increased oxidation arising from exposure to air (the more churning, the greater the reaction with the alcohol in the cask).

Although the wood is old, it has been less affected by its previous contents than are casks previously used for spirits, if only because natural sherry wine is a mere quarter of the strength of newly distilled holandas. Yet the wood is, chemically, rather neutral, so its porosity is crucial. Every house has its own ideas about wood depending upon the final style at which it is aiming. Bobadilla, looking for lightness, uses the newer casks for its cheaper brandy and, once broken in, they are then used for the middle-grade. For their finest brandy, Gran Capitan, Bobadilla uses the well-broken-in casks previously used for its middle-range brandy. The situation is becoming more complicated. Until recent years the brandy makers had been able to rely on an increasing supply of old sherry casks since the vinification of sherry wine has switched from wood to stainless steel. As the Scottish malt whisky distillers have already discovered, the supply of old casks is now diminishing.

The New Laws

At the moment there are no regulations covering Spanish brandy. But a new regulatory system is going through the legislative system, providing a series of minimum criteria for Spanish brandies, detailed on page 114, covering the three categories into which every firm divides its offerings. At the moment virtually every bodega sets its own criteria higher than the new legal minima. These are so low that unscrupulous new entrants could be tempted to undercut the existing houses by making brandy strictly to the legal minimum. But this will help them with only the cheaper brandies. When the regulations become law there will be a tasting panel to judge the organoleptic characteristics of the superior qualities.

Storage and Blending

Like conscientious brandy makers everywhere, the Jerezanos are extremely careful about how and when they reduce the strength of their spirits. They cannot rely on storage to reduce the strength as in Cognac or Armagnac. In theory dry bodegas are bad for brandy. Jerez and Puerto de Santa Maria are near the sea, the relative humidity is fairly high – an average of 65%, ranging up to 95% – so the brandies ought to lose strength rather than quantity over the years. In fact they behave as though they were in dry storage, losing very little strength (probably because the bodegas are warmer than those in the classic French spirit-making regions). So the firms tend to reduce their brandies to near saleable strength early on to help them settle down. Because their basic brands are going to be sold relatively young, they mix the destillado and the holandas, reducing it to 63% before it goes into cask at all. The final reduction to around 40%, just above the strength at which it will be sold, is obviously made in plenty of time, allowing some months for the blend of spirit and water to settle down. For their better brandies (which start weaker because they do not include any destillado, only holandas and alquitara distilled at between 65% and 70%) the spirit is sometimes reduced to 45% before it goes into the solera.

Legally, the brandy can be sold at between 35% and 45% – the range which applied in Gonzalez' day, although, then as now, some was exported at between 58% and 60% to save customs duties by the importing country. In recent years brandies have simultaneously become less strong and less sweet. (A classic case is Terry's Centenario. Originally it was sold at 42%. Ten years ago this was reduced to 40%, now it is sold at 36.5%). Most other brandies are sold at between 37% and 38%, although the premium brands can go up to 40% or more. The range will narrow when the EEC regulations are applied. These will limit strengths to between 37% and 40%.

It is not only strengths which have changed. Until recently there was a fundamental belief in Spain that brandy had to be rich, dark and sweet. This was convenient for the producers, since it enabled them to disguise the underlying rawness of the destillados: "like sugaring the pill for children", says one oenologist. Now, as can be seen from the Directory, even those houses – Osborne is the most obvious example – which offer a traditionally rich style use additives positively, not merely to disguise rawness. In Osborne's case they are designed to provide additional (non-grapey) fruitiness, while most other houses either eschew additives other than the *boisé* used in cognac, or use the richer wines from Jerez itself, like PX, mistelo, and color, the rich wine from Rioja.

Individual examples can be misleading. The variables in Spanish brandy are far greater than those of any other type. The permutations are endless, since they involve the four types of original distillate, the length of storage, the type of wood, the quantities and types of additives. The differences are magnified because most Spanish brandy is sold by half-a-dozen firms. Sometimes it seems that their only stylistic resemblance is in the names they give their finest brandies.

These invariably come from Spain's greatest age, recalling Lepanto, the great sea victory over the Turks, or Pissarro the "Gran Capitan" who conquered Peru, or the warlike Cardenal Mendoza who finally drove the Moors out of Spain, or, less tactfully, the Gran Duque d'Alba whose ruthlessness drove the Dutch subjects of the King of Spain into revolt. The actual brandies, as we shall see, are very different. So, rather than generalize about house styles, it is better to look at them individually.

THE PROPOSED SPANISH BRANDY REGULATIONS

Brandy de Jerez Solera: Six months in wood, 200 mg per 100 of anhydrous matter (800 mg per litre of brandy which weighs 950 grams at 40%).

Brandy de Jerez Solera Reserva: 1 year and 250 mg.

Brandy de Jerez Gran Reserva: 3 yrs 300 mg per 100 cubic cl.

SPAIN

· DIRECTORY ·

The structure of the Spanish brandy business is such that the entries concentrate upon individual companies. These are cross-referenced to the names of their brandies.

The percentage figure after the brand name indicates the proportions it contains of Holandas (H), Destillados (D) and Alquitara (A). If no figures are given it can be assumed that the majority of the brandy in the cheapest blend is destillado, plus some holandas (generally about a third). The second grade will have a majority of holandas and the most expensive is often pure alquitara. The ages quoted are inevitably more vague than is the case with other brandies because of the solera system.

All brandies are 38% in strength and sold in 70 centilitre bottles unless otherwise indicated.

All the houses welcome visitors to their – often remarkable – cellars if given due warning.

SPAIN'S TOP BRANDIES IN 1986* – in '000 cases of 9 litres

	Name	Owner	Quantity
Standard	Soberano	Gonzalez Byass	2050
	Veterano	Osborne	1725
	Centenario	Terry	1150
	103 Blanco	Bobadilla	1100
	Esplendido	Garvey	800
	Fundador	Domecq	500
Medium	Magno	Osborne	925
	Torres	Torres	440
	Carlos III	Domecq	400
Premium	Carlos I	Domecq	45+
	Independencia	Osborne	18
De Luxe	Lepanto	Gonzales Byass	22
	Gran Duque du Alba	Rodegao Internacionales	16
	Cardenal Mendoza	Sanchez Romate	10

Source: International Wine and Spirit Record

ABOLENGO

See Sánchez Romate.

ALFONSO EL SABIO

See Valdespino.

BOBADILLA

Carretera Circunvalacion S/N, Jerez
Tel: (56) 34 86 00
103 White Label (D/H) 3+ · 103 Black Label (A) 5+ · Gran Capitan (A) 25

Bobadilla is a classic family company which managed to maintain the quality of its sherries during the bad years, thanks to the profits from the brandy business which account for 60% of its sales. Fifty years ago Bobadilla introduced a light, dry brandy, then a revolutionary concept. It was typical of the remarkable Don Gonzalo Bobadilla, a trained oenologist, who ran the family firm for 50 years until he retired at the age of 80 in the mid-1970s. His tradition is carried on by his son, Don Xavier Fernandez.

The firm has owned stills in La Mancha for 30 years. Nothing is added to the brandies, before they are aged, to allow the full organoleptic qualities to emerge. In the final blend Bobadilla employs only a little PX and mistelo, both natural products which do not reduce the grapiness of the final product.

The 103 White Label is light, but with enough well-integrated holandas to provide some natural sweetness. The 103 Negro is darker, stronger, heavier, with overtones of nutty toffee and a certain acrid taste as of grape stems. This mellows to a genuine fruity grapiness in the glass.

The Gran Capitan is made from much richer brandies, a quality which is revealed in its depth and creaminess.

BODEGAS INTERNACIONALES

Bodegas Diez-Merito, Apartdao 7, Jerez
Tel: (56) 33 60 54
Gran Duque d'Alba 40% 8+

A brand created by the entrepreneur Jose-Maria Ruiz Mateos by combining the stocks of brandy acquired with the Jerez bodegas he bought up in such numbers in the early 1980s. After the spectacular bankruptcy of his enormous Rumasa empire, and a period under government control, the firm was sold to a mysterious Basque businessman, Marcos Eguizabal.

Inevitably the average age of the brandies in the blend is diminishing as the older brandies pass through the soleras. Gran Duque d'Alba is now made from holandas, bought from outside distillers, and mixed with color and PX. It is a rich, unremarkable, brandy.

CARDENAL CISNEROS

See Sánchez Romate.

CARDENAL MENDOZA

See Sánchez Romate.

CARLOS I

See Domecq.

CARLOS III

See Domecq.

CENTENARIO

See Terry.

CONDE DE OSBORNE

See Osborne.

CONDE DUQUE

See Gonzalez Byass.

DOMECQ

Pedro Domecq, San Ildefonso 3, Jerez 30
Tel: (56) 33 18 00
Fundador (H/D) 3 · Carlos III (A) · Carlos I (A) · Marqués de Domecq (A)

Founded in 1730, Domecq is one of the oldest and most famous of all sherry firms. It was the pioneer of selling brandy – Fundador, first introduced in 1874, is still synonymous with Spanish brandy in many markets. It exports one-third of its output throughout the world, and owns production subsidiaries in four countries. The biggest, in Mexico, dwarfs the parent, producing 7 million cases of brandy annually, making it by far the largest brandy producer in the world. The others are in Colombia (250,000 cases), Brazil (150,000 cases) and Venezuela (100,000 cases).

In Spain Domecq has the largest stock of old brandies, used to great effect in its better brands. Four-fifths of its wine comes from Airén grapes grown in La Mancha, the remaining 20% from the equally unremarkable Jean grape from Terra de Barros. It has 16 pot-stills producing 16,000 litres a day and 5 continuous stills producing 90,000 litres.

Fundador remains a standard for "standard grade" Spanish brandies. Unlike many of its rivals, more than half the blend is holandas. It has a rich feel about it, but no signs of caramel in colour, nose, or palate. Carlos III is lighter than Fundador and greatly resembles a young cognac, for it is obviously the product of a pot-still, but is richer than a cognac of the same age. Carlos I is a smooth, rich, distinctive spirit – although, like all Domecq's brandies, without any hint of artificiality or caramelization.

The finest of all, Marqués de Domecq, is the classic result of the best of modern Spanish practice, showing the full natural sweetness produced by the vinosity of the wood.

DON NARCISO

See Mascaro.

EL CESAR

See Sánchez Romate.

EL SABIO

See Valdespino.

ESPLENDIDO

See Garvey.

ESTILO FINE MARIVAUX

See Mascaro.

FABULOSO

See Palomino y Vergara.

FARAON

See Hidalgo.

FONTENAC

See Torres.

FUNDADOR
See Domecq.

GARVEY
Callé Divina Pastora 3, 11402 Jerez
Tel: (56) 33 05 00
Esplendido 3 · Gran Garvey 5 · Renacimento 20 – all 75 cl
An old sherry company founded in 1780 by an Irishman, William Garvey Power. Claims to have shipped the first Spanish brandy to Britain as far back as 1858. Much later became part of Ruiz Mateos' Rumasa empire. After nationalization it was sold to the German Cooperative AG. It has always bought its holandas from outside distillers. Its cheaper Esplendido brand is run-of-the-mill, rich and sweet, and a success in Spain. Garvey's better brandies are drier and more delicate, more interesting, less successful.

GONZALEZ BYASS
Manuel M. Gonzalez 12, Jerez ***Tel: (56) 34 00 00***
Soberano (D/H) 1 · Insuperable (H/D) 3+ · Conde Duque 5+ · Lepanto (H) 15+
Gonzalez Byass is one of the oldest, best-known sherry firms, one of the handful still controlled by the founding family. Gonzalez' brandies are light, elegant, not typically Spanish. They are all based on the product of their three distilleries, in Tomelloso, La Mancha and in Estremadura. Soberano, Spain's best-selling brandy, which accounts for nearly 90% of Gonzalez' brandy production, exhibits the limitations of a pure brandy made largely from destillado. It has a very oily, "grappaish" nose, without much subtlety or fruit. Insuperable, Gonzalez' entry in the Reserva class, is decidedly darker, oloroso coloured, with a rich, woody, caramelly nose. Long, but with a slightly medicinal finish. Conde Duque is the odd brandy out. A much more orthodox Spanish brandy: rich, with the nose and palate of old-fashioned toffee. Almost medicinally sweet. Gonzalez' pride and joy, Lepanto, deservedly the best-seller at the top end of the market, is pure holandas, some of it from sherry grapes. A very light, clear gold colour, with a well-aged vanilla nose. Rich and oily on the palate, but without fattiness or *rancio*.

GRAN CAPITAN
See Bobadilla.

GRAN DUQUE D'ALBA
See Bodegas Internacionales.

GRAN GARVEY
See Garvey.

GRAN RESERVA
See Torres.

HIDALGO
Vinicola Hidalgo, Banda de la Playa 24, Sanlucar
Tel: (56) 36 05 16
Faraon

Small family business making 4,000 cases of a single prestige brandy, Faraon, sold only in Spain.

IMPERIO
See Terry.

INDEPENDENCIA
See Osborne.

INSUPERABLE
See Gonzalez Byass.

LEPANTO
See Gonzalez Byass.

MAGNO
See Osborne.

MARIVAUX
See Mascaro.

MARQUES DE DOMECQ
See Domecq.

MASCARO
Antonio Mascaro Carbonell, del Casal 9, Villafranca del Penedès, Barcelona ***Tel: (3) 90 16 28***
Estilo Fine Marivaux 1+ · Narciso Etiquette Bleu 3/4 · Don Narciso 8/10
Antonio Mascaro is Spain's most interesting brandy maker, one of only two in Catalonia – the other is the much bigger Torres (qv). Mascaro's father began making brandy in 1945, but concentrated on the cheaper end of the business. The son uses two local grape varieties, the mediocre red Tempranillo and, for his better brandies, the high-acid, fruity Parellada.

The grapes go through continuous presses which extract a lot of the oiliness from the pips. Mascaro distils the wine twice in cognac stills – although they are heated by steam pipes within the stills, not by external heat. He matures his brandies "statically", *à la Charentaise*, in a variety of oak casks (including some resinous wood from the Limousin). The brandies are all richer than their cognac equivalents, but can be remarkably delicate. Even his marc, made partly from Tempranillo, is rich and fine, resembling a Marc de Bourgogne. His cheaper brandy, Estilo Fine Marivaux, is young and a bit raw and *boisé*: the older Narciso Etiquette Bleu already has some vanillin and richness, although young and fiery underneath. Don Narciso is directly comparable to a good 15 year-old cognac. It has a deep rich nose without any of the artificiality implied by the word caramelly. For his own amusement he makes other, even more delicate, brandies which prove that the Parellada can be compared with the Colombard or the Folle Blanche in its suitability for distillation.

MIGUEL I
See Torres.

MIGUEL TORRES
See Torres.

NARCISO
See Mascaro.

1900
See Terry.

103 WHITE LABEL, 103 BLACK LABEL
See Bobadilla.

OSBORNE
Fernan Caballero, Puerto de Santa Maria, Cádiz
Tel: (56) 85 52 11
Veterano 3 · Magno 5 · Independencia 10 · Conde de Osborne (A) 20
A classic family-owned sherry business founded in 1772. As the name implies, the Osbornes were originally British, but in the past two centuries have transformed themselves into the purest Spanish gentlemen, complete with a Papal title conferred by the aged Pius IX in 1869 (the name is now pronounced "Osbornay"). In the 1970s when they ran into financial problems their brandies saved them (particularly the immensely profitable Magno, far and away the market leader for middle-class brandies).

Osborne distils its own brandies through its Jonas Torres subsidiary in Tomelloso. The firm is the strongest believer in non-grape additives. At an early stage in the maturation process macerated plums, almonds, and other unidentified fruits and nuts are added to the brandy. Osborne produces them itself to ensure their purity and quality. What goes into the solera is the final compound, harmonized before maturation, to ensure that the product is well-blended. The air in the bodegas is deliberately kept dry to make certain that the brandy retains its strength.

Not surprisingly, all Osborne's brandies share a house style. The cheaper Veterano still has a young, grappaish nose, with slightly bitter, nut-kernelly overtones. The macerated fruits emerge on the warm palate and leave a nice warm afterglow. Magno has a fruity nose, a nutty fruitiness on the palate and finish, without any bitterness. Independencia offers a much greater intensity of aroma. Rich, nutty, but not caramelly on the palate. Carabela is much richer, evoking a general warmth and nuttiness – like a slightly caramelized armagnac. Conde de Osborne, the family's pride and joy, offered in a peculiar, opaque, blue-grey asymmetrical bottle designed by Salvador Dali, is pure 20-year-old alquitara; and it shows in the rich rancio, its nose and the slightly caramelly richness on the palate.

PALOMINO Y VERGARA
Fabuloso
Old family firm recently taken over by Allied-Lyons after having suffered badly in the hands of Rumasa.

PRIMERO
See Terry.

RENACIMIENTO
See Garvey.

ROMATE
See Sánchez Romate.

SANCHEZ ROMATE
Lealas 26–28, PO Box 5, Jerez *Tel: (56) 33 22 12*
Abolengo 40% 3 · El Cesar 5 · Cardenal Cisneros 12 · Cardenal Mendoza (A) 45%

A small firm, owned by three local families rich enough to go their own way, producing, in Cardenal Mendoza, one of the few Spanish brandies with a world-wide following. It is also the only Jerez firm whose brandies are mostly exported. This is not surprising given their generally high quality. They are all of a piece, very Spanish in the traditional sense. The house style includes a feeling of "olorosoishness" because the casks in which the brandies have been matured previously held oloroso sherry.

Abolengo, the cheapest, has a rather young nose, but a nice feel of milk chocolate on the palate. El Cesar has the authentic Sánchez Romate oloroso nose, and is reminiscent of chocolate caramels on the palate, as does Cardenal Cisneros, which also has a powerful woody-vanilla richness.

The firm's pride and joy is Cardenal Mendoza. It was originally distilled in the 1880s for the owners, their families and friends, and is therefore expressly tailored to the traditional taste of rich – and cultivated – Spanish gentlemen. It has an overwhelming deep, natural sweetness, an equally overwhelming richness, pure distilled oloroso sherry, without any hint of additives. It is double-distilled, immediately reduced to 45%, kept up to five years in individual oak casks before transfer to the soleras – which are composed exclusively of casks which have previously contained oloroso sherries – for the equivalent of another 15 years. Over the past 30 years Cardenal Mendoza has become a cult drink, first in Latin America, then amongst the emigré Cuban community in Florida, next in Spain, and now increasingly in Italy and Germany.

SOBERANO
See Gonzalez Byass.

SOLERA SELECTA
See Torres.

TERRY
Fernando A de Terry SA, Apartado de Correos 30 · Puerto de Santa Marsia *Tel: (56) 86 27 00*
Centenario (D) 1 · 1900 (D/H) 3 · Imperio (H/A) 5 · Primero (H)

Founded in 1883, it immediately started distilling brandies and was an early leader in providing the Spanish with very typically rich brandies. Allied-Lyons, the present owners, have recently relaunched the firm's brandies in new packages.

Terry has had its own stills in Tomalloso for 30 years, including six pot-stills for producing holandas. It started by buying alcohol, went on to found a joint venture and then bought out its partner.

Terry is good at balancing the fruity-nutty esters. They add macerated fruits, but only a few days before the brandy is bottled. Centenario is a classic Spanish-style brandy. Naturally a destillado. The rawness is well masked by toffeeish aromas, also noticeable in the colour, but this gives a nice feel of nut kernels. 1900 is a similar style, some young grappaishness on the nose, but rather cleaner, darker, richer, less nutty than Centenario. Imperio is a deliberately Frenchified brandy, with the aromas of a 3/4 year old cognac, but not as harsh. A pleasant compromise between cognac and coñac. Primero has a nice nutty holandas nose, some richness, a lighter colour than the 1900; again a classic Spanish brandy, rich and bland with warmth and a kick in the tail.

TORRES

Bodegas Miguel Torres, Apartado 13 – Commercio 22, Villafranca del Penedès ***Tel: (89) 00 100***
Torres 5 · Torres 10 Gran Reserva · Fontenac · Solera Selecta · Miguel Torres · Honorable · Miguel I. All are sold in 75 cl bottles at 39.2%, except Miguel I, which is 40.5%.
Visits from 9 am–12 noon and 3–5 pm Monday to Friday.
The biggest and best-known wine-makers in Catalonia. Though the family has been distilling brandy since 1920 it has only recently started making a very wide, and very high-quality, range of brandies based on the high-acid local Parellada grape. This is proving highly suitable for distillation, especially if, like Torres, one uses grapes grown on the slopes of the high Penedès with a mere 8% alcohol. To improve quality, Torres ensures that no sulphur is used in the wine-making, distilling the wines (on their lees to increase richness) only until May.

Torres' wide range of brandies divides into two. The 5 and 10 Torres are both holandas, matured in soleras of American oak. While the 5 Torres is relatively routine, the 10 Torres is already rich and vanilly. The more expensive brandies are all distilled and aged *à la Charentaise*. Fontenac is pure Parellada, distilled (to a mere 61%) with its *secondes* and is consequently a rich, fruity brandy comparable to good VSOP cognac. Miguel Torres, made of Parellada and Ugni Blanc, matured in new oak for six months, has a rich raisinish nose with some caramel from the 1% and 2% of *boisé* used. Miguel I was originally rather *boisé*. It is now purer and naturally rich: while the top blend, Honorable, again a blend of Parellada and Ugni Blanc, has a rich rancioish noise, lots of vanillin, very rich, very earthy, very classy, and very expensive.

VALDESPINO

A.R. Valdespino, Pozo del Olivar 16, PO Box 22, Jerez ***Tel: (56) 33 14 50***
1850 5+ · Alfonso el Sabio 10+. Sold at 40% in 75 cl bottles.
One of the oldest sherry houses. Don Alfonso Valdespino is recorded as having a still and bodega in 1516. The firm still

belongs to his descendants. It buys in brandies (including a little from the local Palomino grapes) and makes a decidedly non-traditional style of brandy. The 1850 is named after the year when a Mr Daniel Wilson, returning to Britain, sold his bodega and its stocks to the family, who still use the bodega and original Limousin oak casks. The 1850 brandy, however, tastes young, with only a little holondas to relieve the destillado. The Alfonso el Sabio is genuine alquitara with a lot of sherry woodiness, some of it rather bitter.

VETERANO
See Osborne.

PORTUGAL

The Portuguese should be able to make brandies as good as anyone in the world since they have a ready supply of acid white grapes for their famous Vinho Verde. Unfortunately, only a few firms (most notably Avelada) have realized this potential. There is some excuse for the Oporto-based port merchants who are mostly handling black (or sugary white) grapes, but there is no such excuse for the firms based in Anadia in the heart of Vinho Verde country. Too often they use for brandy the Baga, a thick-skinned astringent black grape, used to make the most of the Bairrada and some Dão wines. Most firms make a marc (bagaceira) of just above 40%, as well as a brandy (aguardente) generally of 39%.

ALIANCA

Caves Alianca
VS Antiqua · VSOP · Antiquissima
The VS has a light agreeable nose, a good pure light colour, a little richness, but still comparable to a 4–5 year old cognac. The VSOP is much richer and more caramelly, while the Antiquissima is even richer with more complex nose.

AVELADA

Estate: Sociedade Agricola e Comercial da Quinta de Avelada, 4560 Penafiel ***Tel: (55) 22041/2/3***
Offices: Rua Sa da Bandeira 819–20, 4002 Porto
Tel: (2) 381350/317247
Bagaceira 41% · Adega Velha 39% 70 cl 10+
A major family estate and one of the biggest producers of Vinho Verde. Over the past 16 years the family has taken advantage of this to become a serious major producer of brandies – and ages more than it currently sells. Buys Loureiro, Trajadura, Pedernão and Azal grapes from all over the Vinho Verde region. Uses a recently bought continuous still to make marc and a large (35hl) equally new cognac still to make brandy. The spirit is aged in Limousin oak casks. The brandy, from low-alcohol, acid wines, is relatively dark and heavy, but its sweetness is natural, most appealing and grapey. Avelada's bagaceira is full of an equally natural grapey sweetness.

BORLIDO

Caves Borlido Apartado 10, Sangalhos, 3780 Anadia
Tel: (34) 741512
Aguardente Velha 38% 3 · Aguardente Velhissima 38% 5
A major wine producer and merchant in Bairrada. Founded in 1930 and five years later started producing brandies. Uses Nacerao and Bica Alberta grapes. Now has two new substantial continuous stills each producing a hectolitre an hour at 77%. The spirit is immediately diluted with hot water and then aged in 600 to 800 litre oak casks.

CONSTANTINO

4400 Vila Nova de Gaia ***Tel: 300866***
Brandy Constantino 3–5

The brandy subsidiary of Ferreira, the well-known firm of port shippers. It is the second largest brandy seller in Portugal, buying young brandies from Estremadura and ageing them in wood.

DALVA
See Da Silva.

DA SILVA
C. da Silva, 247 Rua Felizardo de Lima, PO Box 30, 4401 Vila Nova de Gaia ***Tel: 394128***
Dalva: XXXXX 3 · VO 12 · VSOP 30
Da Silva: 10 years old
Saint-Clair 40
The Douro Fathers 10
Mainly a port producer. Its brandies, which account for a fifth of its turnover, are bought from the Portuguese state monopoly.

IMPERIO
Caves Imperio, Apartado 9, Sanghalos, 3783 Anadia ***Tel: (34) 741204***
Bagaceira Fina 48% · Bagaceira Paraiso 41% · Bagaceira Zimbreira 48% · Imperio VSOP 4 · Reliquia 6 · Mousinho · Aguardente Velha · Anniversario Reserva Especial 20
Major firm, still controlled by some of the six families who founded it in 1942. They double distil the wines, which would otherwise be used for sparkling wines, and then age the brandies in 5,000 litre oak casks. One of the most dedicated Portuguese brandy makers.

MOUSINHO
See Imperio.

NIEPOORT
Rua Infante D Henrique 39–20, 4000 Oporto
Tel: 21028
Brandy 3 · Casteles 3 · Aguardente Velha 25
A port firm which sells a little aguardente aged in port casks.

NETO COSTA
Caves Neto Costa, Apartado 13, 3781 Anadia
Tel: (34) 52013/4
Aguardente Bagaceira Grappa Marc 50% · XXXXX Old Brandy 5 · Aguardente Velha 38% 8 · VSOP Fine Old Brandy 10
Started producing sparkling wines and liqueurs in 1931, and only added still wines and brandies to its range in the 1940s. Buys in powerful grappa/bagaceira/marc, but for its brandies it buys local wines (mostly, presumably, Baga) from Bairrada and distils them in a small (8 hectolitre) Charentais still, ageing them in oak casks of varying sizes. The result, says the firm, is brandies which are: "of light colour, dry to your taste, smooth but not too scented".

PALACIO DA BREJEIRA
Maria Herminia D'Oliviera Paes, Palacio da Brejeira, Pinheiros, 4950 Moncao ***Tel: 56129***
Aguardente Velha · Aguardente de Bagaco (Bagaceira)
The D'Oliviera family originally distilled brandies to use up the "vins de presse" discarded when making their wine. They describe their bagaceira as a: "suigeneris 'aguardente' with a caste flavour and with a very low content of methylic alchool". Despite Madame D'Oliveira's inadequate English she is making a serious brandy, using only her own grapes, otherwise used for vinho verde. These are distilled in a new continuous still and then matured in small (700 litres) French oak for at least seven years.

PARAISO
See Imperio.

QUINTA DO RIBEIRINHO
Amoreira da Gandara, 3780 Anadia
Tel: (34) 58156/96432
The Moreira Pires e Pato family started distilling the lees from its white wines in 1962. M. Luis Alberto began selling it in 1970. The grapes are washed so that the lees have plenty of sugar in them. They are distilled twice in a small (4 hl) cognac-type still, and then kept in 600 litre oak casks for seven years or more. The result, say the owners, is "oaky but smooth".

RELIQUIA
See Imperio.

Rittos, Irmaos, Rua Padre Antonio Vieira 68, 4300 Porto ***Tel: (2) 50864/51377/560624***
Brandy · Brandy VO (numbered bottles)
Brandies produced by well-known port shippers.

SAINT-CLAIR
See Da Silva.

SAO DOMINGO
Caves do Solar de Sao Domingos, Apartado 16, 3781 Anadia ***Tel: (34) 3152068***
Brandy 36% · Bagaceira 46% · Aguardente Velha 42% 2 · Aguardente Velhissima 41% 5
Established in 1942, originally to make sparkling wines and brandies. Its bagaceira is famous in Lisbon: its "brandy" is a young brew sweetened with sugar; the other brandies are mostly distilled in its own continuous still, from bought-in Baga wines and aged in oak. It buys in its bagaceiras from local distillers.

ZIMBREIRA
See Imperio.

ITALY

Italy has two quite different traditions for distilled spirits. One is industrial, expressed in the handful of firms built up over the last century who make both brandy and grappa – the Italian equivalent of marc. The other is the peasant tradition of thriftily using the marc from their grapes, and the lees from their wines, to make their own grappas.

Neither brandy nor grappa has been overly successful recently. Until 1983 their makers were sheltered from external competition, for excise duties on imported spirits were far higher than those on native products. Eventually the EEC forced them to be levelled, and the Italians have now turned to a greater variety of spirits – notably malt whisky. Sales of brandy in Italy – which had already started to fall before the taxes were levelled – declined from 4 million cases in 1979 to 3.3 million in 1985. Exports, at less than a million bottles, are not much help. Grappa sales have gone down at much the same rate, from 3.8 million cases in 1979 to 3.2 million in 1985, and, unless the bigger firms can mount more successful export efforts, they are likely to decline further since they can offer no great originality to a market which increasingly demands exceptional products.

Brandy

Italians point to the Piedmontese word "branda" to show that their brandies have historic origins. In fact they, like the Spanish, owe their start as large-scale makers of brandy to the phylloxera which hit Cognac before some of the Mediterranean wine regions – indeed until 1948 the Italians called their brandies "cognac". Brandy is a closely controlled appellation in Italy, supervised by a separate brandy institute. Fortunately, given the scandals which have afflicted Italian wines, the regulations covering brandy resemble those for pharmaceutical, rather than other alcoholic products. The wines, which may originate only from specified areas, are analysed before distillation; they can be distilled only to a relatively low maximum strength to ensure that the fruitiness of the original grape is retained; brandy must be aged for at least one year – younger spirit, sold only in Italian bars, is called acquavite, distillato or (a phrase used by the poet D'Annunzio) arzente; additives are strictly limited to caramel and one percent of a sweetening agent. The ages quoted for Italian brandies are those of the youngest spirit in the blend. The government also encourages quality by giving progressively greater tax reliefs the longer the brandy is kept. A one-year-old gets 18% relief, a figure which rises to 88% for an eight-year-old (few Italian brandies are sold much older since they then become overly tannic). Nevertheless Italian brandy, while of a generally high standard (partly because its production is concentrated in so few hands) is not remarkable. It is easy to drink, but can be relatively bland and lacks character.

Brandy Firms

The market is dominated by two firms, Buton and Stock, which together account for 1.7 million cases. Another dozen or so makers account for most of the rest. Despite the tax incentives it is not, in general, a well-aged product, since stocks amount to only 10 months' consumption. It is still seasonal, with nearly half the total sold in the run-up to Christmas.

BUTON

Viale Angelo Masini 24, 40126 Bologna
Tel: (51) 359672.
Vecchia Romagna Etichetta Nera · Vecchia Romagna Etichetta Oro · Vecchia Romagna Etichetta Bianca

INGA

Via Garibaldi 10, 1–15069 Seravalle Scrivia
Tel: (143) 65965
Inga 1–3 · Riserva Impero 36% 7+
An old-established family firm originaly called Gambarotta (the name was sold to Buton (qv) in 1982). It uses marc and wine, 90% Barbera and 10% Dolcetto, distilled continuously, then stored in oak casks holding between 400 and 10,000 litres.

ORO PILLA

See Pilla.

PILLA

Via Ronco 1, Castelmaggiore, Bologna
Tel: (51) 700235
Oro Pilla White Shield 2+ · Scudo Nero Black Shield 5+ · Gold Shield 8+
The firm, founded in the Veneto in 1920, originally became famous for its aperitif Select. In 1954 a new owner, Leonida Zarri, moved the firm to a splendid country house near Bologna where he created a number of wines and spirits, including three brandies which are now the fourth best-selling range in Italy.

STOCK

Via Lionello Stock 2, Trieste 34100
Tel: (40) 414181
'84 Originale · '84 VSOP · XO
In 1884 Lionello Stock formed a cooperative of distillers in Trieste to take advantage of the shortage of cognac caused by the phylloxera. Reliance on Central and Eastern European markets proved disastrous, but since the war Stock has bounced back remarkably well all over the world.

The brandy is single-distilled in externally heated (gas-fired), cognac-type stills. The '84 VSOP, the basic brand, is wood-aged for four years. It has a light orange-yellow colour, a nice mature, grapey nose and has vanilla on the palate, with some fire on the aftertaste. In some markets Stock sells an XO, which is rich and not overly caramelly, a good blend of "fire and velvet", as well as eight and 10 year old blends.

VECCHIA ROMAGNA

See Buton.

Grappa

Grappa was originally a peasant drink, designed to provide comfort and strength to the maker – usually a poor peasant in the mountains of northern Italy – who also found it a sovereign remedy against the depression which accompanies old age. It was so strong that even a few drops in a cup of coffee gave one new life.* Since the war the best of them have become (deservedly) cult drinks. This is partly snobbery, parallel to the general acceptance of former exclusively peasant foods, such as gnocchi or tagliatelle, reflecting the search after older traditions by self-conscious urban intellectuals. To be fair, it also reflects the way in which the peasant tradition can, at its best, preserve the essential qualities of some of Italy's finest, if sometimes neglected, grape varieties (like the Arneis, distilled separately by Marolo, amongst others).

Grappa was always a regional drink. Even the name varies. In the Veneto, indeed in any region which was formerly part of the Austro-Hungarian Empire, it is called sgnappa, in Piedmont branda the same as in France. Only the Lombards (romantics like Luigi Veronelli),† were faithful to the Italian name for grape and called it grappa. The most famous grappas come from Bassano, the town dominated by Monte Grappa, a hill allegedly impregnated with its smell. Local wines proved suitable for distillation, and the Venetian proletariat came to like Bassano grappa as a digestif; it was recommended as a medicine, even a disinfectant. These varied uses turned Bassano into the major centre for grappa production, dominated by Nardini (qv).

Today sales are increasingly concentrated with northern Italy taking over 90% of the grappa sold in Italy. "Industrial" grappas are divided into two types, Pregiate (premium) and Correnta (standard/normal). In recent years the nationally promoted, more expensive Pregiate brands have been losing ground in a price war to the regional Correnta brands which now have three-fifths of the market. By no coincidence, sales are increasingly concentrated in supermarkets which now account for two-thirds of all sales.

The older type of peasant distiller could produce a remarkable product, partly because there were no real rules covering grappa. A few *consorzi* in northern Italy have tried to impose their own, regional, regulations, but only the inhabitants of the Trentino have had any great success. Elsewhere, only the producer's name provides any guarantee of quality. The northern Italians, sprinkling the lees with water, produce a liquid of some 4 to 5% suitable for distillation (One reason why other regions, which also make grappa, produce an inferior product is because their mechanical presses are so efficient that the raw material contains only 2 to 2.5% alcohol). One needs 15 to 20 kilos of even the best marc to produce a single hectolitre of wine – the marc is about 47% grape skins, 28% stalk, 18 to 30% seed, a proportion reflected in the quality of the marcs.

* It can also be "tasted" by rubbing a little into the palm of the hand, as though it were perfume, or by letting a few drops fall into a cup of boiling water.

† His analyses in the *Catalogo Bolaffi delle Grappe*, published by Guilio Bolaffi, have proved invauable in writing this section.

The peasant distiller can use fresh local marcs (they should not be more than a day old, says Veronelli, so the stills should not be more than 10 kilometres from the winery). Since most wine makers are naturally trying to maximize the amount of juice they can extract from their grapes, it requires a particularly conscientious grower to ensure there is enough sugar in the marc.

Grappa can be made either in pot-stills or, more frequently, in bain-maries, the *calendres* used in Champagne. The key to quality is not only the speedy collection, and thus the freshness of the marcs, but also the slowness of distillation to ensure the extraction of the maximum amount of sugar from the marcs, and that the heads and tails are cut. Pot-stills, providing lower degrees of distillation, and therefore less rectification and better control of the process, are ideal, but possible only for *artisanal* grappa.

The final styles depend partly on the method of distillation, partly on the grape varieties, and partly on the region. The Trentino grappas are reputed young, lively and fresh, those from Piedmont dry, full-bodied and strong (thus resembling, say the locals, their own dialect), those from the Veneto dense and velvety, promising more than they deliver, while those from Friuli are lively and rounded. These styles are also affected by the sharp distinction between grappas bottled and sold almost immediately after distillation and thus, hopefully, retaining the fruitiness of the original marc, and those kept in casks of oak (occasionally acacia) for up to seven years.

Grappa Firms

There are hundreds of firms making grappa. I have selected only the largest as well as a handful of the more *artisanal* concerns which typify their regions.

BAROZZI ERNESTO

Lizzana di Rovereto ***Tel: (46) 433713***
Grappa Riserva 40% · Graspamara 40%
Both stored for three years in oak casks. The Riserva is a highly rated Trentino-type grappa.

BERTOLO

Lorenzo Bertolo, Via del Carmine 2 bis, 10122 Torino ***Tel: (11) 512400***
Grappa di Moscato 43% · Grappa Stravecchia 43% · Taurinese 42%
A family company which has added a range of grappas bought ready-bottled "from an old distiller" in Piedmont.

BOCCHINO

Distilleria Canaellese, Via G.B. Guiliani 30, Canelli ***Tel: (14) 182266***
Sigillo Nero 42% · Grappa Gran Moscato 42% · Grappa di Nebbiolo 42% · Grappa della Grappa Cantina Privata 45%
One of the biggest Grappa makers. The cheapest Sigillo Nero is made from Piedmont wines, the two varietals are unexceptionable, while the top-of-the-range Cantina Privata is made from Muscat and Barbera.

CANDOLINI

Via Fatebenefratelli 4/A, Gorizia ***Tel: (4) 812681***
Grappa Argento 43% · Grappa alla Ruta 45% · Grappa Tokaj 42% · Grappa Gran Riserva 40%
All Candolini's grappas are from grapes grown on the east side of the hills around Friuli, all made in pot-stills by the firm itself. The Gran Riserva is considered to be a particularly subtle grappa.

CARPENE MALVOTI

Via Carpene 1, Conegliano Veneto ***Tel: (43) 823531***
Grappa Vecchia 45%
One of Italy's best-selling grappas, made from grapes from the Veneto,.stored for three years in Limousin oak. Intense but thought a little unclean because of the need to remove the methyl alcohol.

SCOULA ENOLOGICA DI CONEGLIANO

Via Zamboni 8, Conegliano (TV) ***Tel: (43) 823248***
Acquavite di Vinaccia 50%
A model Venetan grappa, made from the local grapes, distilled by the local oenological academy.

DISTILLERIA CERETTO

Localita Moretto Treiso d'Alba
Grappa di Dolcetto 45% · Grappa di Nebbiolo 50%
Two of Italy's most distinguished grappas. Distilled either in a bain-marie or in pot-stills, from a variety of local grapes; sold five months after distillation. The Dolcetto is held to be elegant, the Nebbiolo intense and dry, reflecting the best qualities of Piedmontese wines.

DALMATO-FRIULANA DEI MARCHESI RICCI

Via Nazionale, Magnano in Riviera ***Tel: (43) 279289***
Sgnape Furlane di Ramandul
One of the best oak-aged grappas from Friuli.

DELLA MORTE DISTILLERIE

Via della Contea 23, Pedemonte Valpolicella
Tel: (45) 681088
Grappa Pedemonte DM1 40% · Grappa Pedemonte DM3 43%
The DM1, from the local grapes used to make Valpolicella and stored in stainless steel, is a good example of a typical Venetan grappa. The DM3 is kept in oak for four years and is inevitably more fragrant and intense.

FATTOR ANGELO

Ronchia di Faedis Udine ***Tel: (432) 728094***
Grappa di Faedis 50%
A typical Friuli grappa, kept in stainless steel.

LANDY

Via Buozzi 1, Rastignano di Pianoro (BO)
Tel: (51) 744444
Grappa la Piave 42% · Piave Ruta 42%
Best-selling grappas from the Veneto, kept in oak for two years, but otherwise unremarkable.

LUNGAROTTI

Cantine G. Lungaritto, Via Mario Angeloni 16,06039 Torginao ***Tel: (75) 982348***
Grappa di Rubesco 45%
This famous family firm of wine makers has a limited amount of the lees of its Sangiovese and Canaiolo grapes distilled into marc, which it sells after a few months in bottle.

MAGNOBERTA DISTILLERIE

Via Asti 6, Casale Monferrato (AL) ***Tel: (1) 422022***
Raspa d'Oro Gran Riserva 43% · Acquavite Stravecchia 60%
The cheaper Raspa d'Oro is a decent, typically Piedmontese grappa. The Acquavite, helped by its strength, is extraordinarily intense.

MAROLO

Distilleria Santa Teresa dei Fratelli Marolo, Case Sparse 35, Mussotto d'Alba (CN) ***Tel: (17) 334963***
Di Dolcetto 48% · Di Nebbiolo 49% · Di Barolo · Di Arneis 53%
Three distinguished (and expensive) Piedmontese grappas made by a family firm, presented with what must be the prettiest of all grappa labels. The brothers take great care to distil each variety separately, without stalks, using their own bain-maries. The Nebbiolo is matured in wood for six months, but the Barolo, as befits the grape, is matured in acacia or oak casks for 10 years. The most unusual, the Arneis, is made from a much-cherished local grape of considerable depth and fruitiness which reminds some connoisseurs of pears.

MASCHIO MARCELLO

Distilleria Agricola viale Madonna, Motta di Livenza (TV) ***Tel: (42) 276008***
Goccia d'Oro 42% · Grappa di Cabernet 60%
Excellent examples of Venetan grappas. The Goccia d'Oro is made from Tokay and Merlot, and kept for seven years in oak in a temperature-controlled cellar. The Cabernet, one of the few spirits made from this grape, is kept for 10 years and shows its age in its mellowness.

MASI

S Ambroglio di Valpolicella (VR) ***Tel: (45) 681696***
Grappa di Recioto Mezzanella 50%
Grappa made from Recioto Mezzanella, kept for one to six years in oak and acacia casks.

NARDINI BORTOLO

Ponte Vecchio, Bassano del Grappa
Tel: (42) 422104
Acquavite Bianca 50% · Acquavite Riserva 50% · Acquavite alla Ruta 43%
Founded in 1779 by Bartolo Nardini who bought a house on the end of the bridge across the Po in Bassano. He thus attracted the passing traffic on its way to and from Venice who bought his – then cheap – grappa. He has always been the biggest concern in the town.

Today Nardini's Bianca is sold soon after distillation; the Riserva is kept for three years in oak, while the Alla Ruta is flavoured with stalks of sweet-smelling grasses.

NONINO

Via Acquileia 104, Percuto (UD) ***Tel: (432) 676333***
Acquavite Sauvignon 45% · Acquavite Sauvignon Optima 45% · Acquivite Sauvignon alla Genziana 45% · Acquivite Sauvignon al Ginepro 45% · Acquavite Sauvignon alla Ruta 45% · Vuisinar 45% · Di Ribolla 45% · Di Schioppettino 45% · Di Picolit 52%
Makers of one of the widest ranges of Grappas, mostly from the white grapes of the Friuli hills. The acquavites, some of them flavoured with macerated roots or herbs, are less interesting than the Vuisinar which is kept for up to five years in casks of wild cherry wood (from the local forests). The three individual grappas are stored only in glass. The Picolit, in particular, is a much sought-after grappa.

RAMAZOTTI DISTILLERIE

Via Ramazotti 2, Lainate (MI) ***Tel: (2) 9377***
Fior di Vite 41% · Fior di Vite Bianca 42%
Cheap, widely distributed "industrial" grappas made by a subsidiary of the French Pastis firm, Pernod-Ricard.

SANDRI FIORENTINO

Localita Molini, Faedo (TN)
Grappa Molini 48%
An unusual grappa strongly reminiscent of the Müller-Thurgau from which it is made.

SGNAPE FURLANE DI RAMANDUL

See Dalmato-Friulana dei Marchesi Ricci.

SIBONA DOMENICO

Via Roma 10, Piobesi d'Alba (CN) ***Tel: (173) 619629***
Grappa Finissima della Langa 49% · Grappa di Nebbiolo 42% · Grappa di Nebbiolo Invecchiata 42% · Grappa di Nebbiolo Nature Dry 48% · Grappa di Nebbiolo Tuttogrado 60% · Grappa di Barbaresco 52% · Grappa di Arneis 49%
Makers of a wide range of relatively ordinary multi-varietals. The Arneis (a much cherished variety) and Barbaresco are both splendid examples of single-varietal grappas sold young. The Barbaresco is considered exceptionally well-balanced.

STOCK

Via Lionello Stock 2, Trieste ***Tel: (40) 414181*** **Julia**
One of the biggest brandy producers in Italy. Julia is a relatively ordinary, but best-selling, grappa made from grapes from the Trentino and the Veneto.

VAL DI ROSE

Tenuta Villanova, Via Contessa Beretta 7, 34070 Farra d'Isonzo Gorizzia ***Tel: (481) 888013***
Val di Rose · Acquavite di Uve Traminer

A small family-owned firm distilling since 1932. The grappas are matured for one year in oak casks holding between five and 10 hectolitres.

ZANI

Via Cividale 7, Faedis (UD) ***Tel: (432) 728046***

Grappa Fruiliana di Faedis Stravecchia 45%

An excellent Friuli grappa kept for five years in oak.

ZENI

Azienda Agricola di A & R Zeni, Via Lungo Adige Grumo di San Michele all'Adige (TN)

Tel: (4) 663456

Acquavite di Vinaccia di Teroldego 48%

An excellent Trentino grappa, made from the local grapes and sold young.

GERMANY (AND AUSTRIA)

Of all the widely sold brandies in the world, the German is the least authentic. Because virtually every native German grape is used more profitably to make as much wine as possible, brandies are made exclusively from wines imported, either from Italy, or from France. Many of these, ironically, come from the Cognac region and have already been fortified to about 23%. This fortification keeps them stable but removes the final product yet further from any of the tastes or aromas associated with the original raw material.

German brandies may not be authentic, but they are perfectly wholesome and well regulated. They are distilled either in pot or continuous stills. Standard blends must be aged in containers of not more than 1,000 litres for at least six months and older brandies (Alter Weinbrand – AW in the text – or Uralt) for not less than a year. Additives include the usual range of caramel, *boisé*, and macerated fruits and nuts. The result is that German brandies resemble the less exciting type of Spanish brandy.

In 1985 – when total sales of 11.2 million cases were down only 900,000 on the 1979 figure – native German brandies accounted for 8.9 million cases, cheap imports from France, Spain and Greece for a further 1.3 million cases, while only 855,000 cases of cognac were sold. Because the business is concentrated in only a few hands the entries are grouped under the name of the firm marketing the brands.

There are a number of low-strength (32%) Brandy Verschnitts on sale. Normal brandies are sold at 38% in bottles of 70 cl unless otherwise indicated.

ASBACH

Am Rottland 2–10, 6220 Rüdesheim
Asbach Uralt (AW)

Founded by Hugo Asbach, who in 1907 started using the word weinbrand, which since 1971 has been the official name for all German brandy. Asbach Uralt is by far the biggest premium brand in the German market selling 17 million bottles annually. It is made from fortified wines, imported from Cognac and Armagnac, and then distilled either in pot-stills or continuously in four "factories", two in Germany and one each in France and Italy. It is aged for a year in small oak casks and then for six months more in larger wooden vats. According to James Long it is then: "flavoured with prune juice and extracts of green almond shells".

ATTACHE

See Eckes.

BOLS

Lucas Bols, Graf-Landsbergstrasse 3–5
Tel: (202) 524252
Bols Alter Weinbrand

Subsidiary of the Dutch liquor group. It buys wine from

France and Italy, as well as "maybe Germany". Distils it in five pot-stills and one continuous still.

BON CHERI
See Spitz.

CHANTRE
See Eckes.

GUSTAV DECKER
Postfach 1260, Schlachhofstrasse 14, D–6740 Landau/Pfalz *Tel: (6341) 4001*
Kaiserberg 2 · Dupont Alter Weinbrand · VSOP 3 · Steinalter 7
Family company owned by Heinz and Rut Steiner which has been distilling since 1860. Buys French and Italian wines to distil in its four pot-stills, each holding 50 hectolitres. Ages its brandies far longer than any other German firm. The basic Kaiserberg has rather a raw young nose. But it is quite spicy on the palate, with a fruitcake warmth. The Dupont is less raw, with some grapiness, but the overwhelming feel on the palate is a generalized toffee-like sweetness. The Steinalter is good and grapey, slightly medicinal, fiery on the finish.

DIPLOMAT
See Spitz.

DUJARDIN
See Racke.

DUPONT
See Gustav Decker.

ECKES
D–6501 Nieder-Olm *Tel: (06136) 350*
Attache · Chantre · Mariacron (AW)
Established in 1857 and still a family group. The biggest firm in German brandy. Now depends on two brands, Chantre, introduced in 1953, named after the wife of the then chairman, Ludwig Eckes, and Mariacron, one of the biggest selling brandies in the world. This was named after a monastery acquired by the family in 1961. Eckes' brandies are continuously distilled, and aged for six to 12 months in 350-litre Limousin casks. Mariacron, bland, but with a lot of warmth, is an excellent mixing brandy.

KAISERBERG
See Gustav Decker.

MARIACRON
See Eckes.

MELCHERS RAT
See Racke.

MEISTERBRAND
See Scharlachberg.

NORIS
See Pabst & Richarz.

PABST & RICHARZ
An der Weinkaje, D–2887 Elsfeth *Tel: (4404) 5010*
Noris Dreistern · Tisserand · Stueck 1826 · Tisserand VSOP(AW) · Prestige · Pfalzer Weinbrand
Old-established family firm, founded in 1861. It buys wines from France, Italy, Spain and Greece and distils them either in its three steam-heated pot-stills or one externally heated pot-still. These are then blended with other spirit distilled to not more than 86%. Before bottling the brandies are flavoured with up to 1% of sugar, caramel and an infusion of plums. Its Pfalzer Weinbrand is the only German brandy I have been able to trace which is made from native grapes; an authentic German product.

RACKE
Stefan-George Strasse 20, Postfach 207, 6530 Bingen-Rhein *Tel: (6721) 1880*
Dujardin Imperial VSOP (Alter Weinbrand) · Dujardin Golden Keys · Melcher's Rat.
A major German wine and spirits firm buying its wines from Cognac and double-distilling them in ten 20-hectolitre stills. Imperial, its biggest-selling brand, offers a bland, attractive blend of caramel and grapiness. Racke also sells a blended brandy in Austria: Golden Keys is sold exclusively to NATO. Melcher's Rat is a subsidiary brand going to the grocery trade.

SPITZ
Bernaschkeplatz 3, 4041 Linz *Tel: (7322) 313360*
Bon Cheri · Diplomat · Diplomat VSOP (AW)
A major, long-established Austrian firm, founded in 1857 and now making and marketing a wide range of food and drinks.

STEINALTER
See Gustav Decker.

STUECK
See Pabst & Richarz.

TISSERAND
See Pabst & Richarz.

RUSSIA AND EASTERN EUROPE

Ordinary: XXX 3 · XXXX 4 · XXXXX 5
Branded: KB 6–7 · KBBK 8–10 · KC 10+
"Collection" brandies are branded brandies matured for a further three years in wood.

The Russians and the inhabitants of Eastern Europe concentrate on brandies made out of plums and other orchard fruits rather than from grapes, but a wide variety of brandies is also made from grapes – in Russia the pre-Revolutionary word conac is still used to describe brandy made out of wine. (In Yugoslavia brandy is known, more correctly, as *vinjak*).

The Russians claim that they have been distilling grapes for 200 years. Certainly the first industrial distillery was established in Georgia in 1886 and before the Revolution others were built in all the Russian grape-growing and wine-making provinces around the Black Sea and in the Caucasus. The Communists continued the tradition, and the latest estimate is that, despite the Gorbachev antispirit campaign, about 100 million litres are sold annually – which puts the Russians into the first division of brandy producers.

Brandies in Russia (and indeed throughout Eastern Europe) are distilled from local grape varieties. These include the Rkatsiteli, a floral grape with high acidity, and the more flowery Mtsvane and Dimiat. In Russia the brandies are matured for at least three years in casks made from oak grown in southern Russia and are then blended with sugar, caramel, older brandies and what are described as "alcoholised and fragrant waters".

BULGARIA

Pliska 3–5 · Pomorie 5+ · Preslav 7+ · Pliska 1300 12+ · Pliska Aheloy 12+ · Great Preslav 17+ · Black Sea Gold 17+

The Bulgarians have followed the same policy with brandy as they have done so successfully with wines since the war: they have concentrated on the mass application of modern standards and techniques to produce acceptable, very low-cost, but technically correct and acceptable products. The brands are named after three major towns in the brandy region of eastern Bulgaria: Pliska and Preslav, both formerly medieval capital cities, and Pomorie on the Black Sea coast.

The Bulgarians claim they started distilling wines in 1945. However it was only in 1954 that they started selling their first brand, Pliska (since this is sold at any time after its third birthday they probably began distilling in 1951, presumably using grapes from vines planted immediately after the war). Pliska became so popular that the name is now virtually synonymous with brandy. The wines are made from Ugni Blanc and two white wine varieties, Dimiat and Rkatziteli, without sulphur dioxide, and distilled to not more than 70% alcohol, thus maintaining the final quality of all the brandies. These are then distilled in one of four ways: in a pot-still, either twice *à la Charentaise*; in a single pass, similar to the process used for alquitara in Spain (qv); or in two types of continuous distillation column, the larger with a purification and concentration column.

The brandy is then matured in cellars at Preslav and Pomorie, which give their names to the better brands. All the brandies are aged for at least three years in oak casks, holding 200 to 300 litres, made from *Quercus sessiflora* – Winter Oak – a local variety grown in the Strandja mountains and the eastern part of the Balkan hills. When the distillate has been reduced to its selling strength (between 40% and 42%) it is allowed to settle for as long as one year in large oak casks holding up to 80 hectolitres.

CYPRUS

ADONIS
See SODAP.

FIVE KINGS
See Keo.

KEO
Franklyn Roosevelt Avenue No 1, PO Box 209, Limassol ***Tel: (51) 62053***
Cocktail 36% "Young" · VO 38% 3 · Extra 39% 8 · VSOP 12 · Five Kings 65cl "Blend of very old brandy"
One of the oldest Cypriot wineries, originally established in 1927 on the slopes of the Troodos mountains. Its brandies are made from local grape varieties, double-distilled in two splendid old pot-stills, complete with big rectifying vessels. Keo owns a bewildering variety of storage vessels, ranging from 11 massive 500 hectolitre vats to 800 Charentais-size casks of 205 litres each. All are made of Limousin oak. Up to 1% of sugar is added just before bottling.

SODAP
PO Box 6314, Limassol ***Tel: (51) 64605***
Sodap VO 5 · Sodap VSOP 15+ · Adonis VSOP 15+
The biggest cooperative on the island. It is best known for its Kolossi brand wines but has also made brandies from the local grape varieties since it was founded in 1947. It has three continuous stills of its own, and distils 70% of the wines from the cooperative's 10,000 members. The distillates are then matured in 500 litre French oak casks, cut with distilled water, stored in large wood vessels and sold, Sodap claims, without any additives.

Traditionally, virtually all American brandy has been distilled in the San Joaquin Valley, not itself famous for its wines. Before Prohibition the brandies were often made from classic cognac varieties like the Colombard and the Ugni Blanc, but the new industry which grew up after 1934 relied more upon the prolific but neutral Thompson Seedless. Most of today's brandies are continuously distilled, and then diluted to around 50% before maturation in American oak casks.

The regulations covering the spirit are, theoretically, rigid – nowadays only grapes grown in California may be used. These permit brandy makers to use up to 2.5% of "rectifying agents" including caramel, liquid sugar, prune juice and other fruit extracts and fortified wines. Usually the casks used have previously contained Bourbon whiskey, which helps to increase the richness. In this, as in many other ways, Californian brandies have some resemblance to their Spanish counterparts, being designed for consumption by a public with a sweet tooth.

Spanish brandies, however, are designed to be drunk neat, while the best-selling Californian brandies are advertised as "a one-bottle bar", more suitable for mixing than for sipping straight.

The turmoil in the American spirits industry is now such that even the biggest companies seem unsure which, if any, distilleries they own and what brandies they make. Many of the companies produce superior brandies with a higher than usual proportion of pot-still brandy. Recently a handful of newcomers, notably Woodbury and RMS (Rémy Martin), have deliberately made double-distilled spirit from classic cognac-style grapes.

CEREMONY
See Guild.

CHRISTIAN BROTHERS
The Christian Brothers (Mont La Salle Vineyards), PO Box 391, St Helena, CA 94574
Tel: (707) 963 4480
Until the Gallos crashed into the market, the best-selling American brandy was made by the Christian Brothers as part of their wide range of drinks. They claim to hold the biggest stock of brandy in the USA in their cellars at Reedley in the San Joaquin Valley. They buy in their grapes (85% Thompson Seedless), ferment them to a mere 7% and distil them in two continuous stills and two pot-stills. Their standard brand is typical, clean, light, with a hint of sweetness. Their XO Aged Premium Brandy, about half pot-still, is oaky and fragrant.

CRESTA BLANCA
See Guild.

CRIBARI
See Guild.

GALLO

E & J Gallo Winery, PO Box 1130, Modesto, CA 95353.

In replying to our questionnaire the Gallo brothers, Ernest and Julius, fully lived up to their reputation for secrecy. They would tell us only that their brandy, E & J, is the best seller in the USA and is made in two continuous stills. In fact it is a light, rather bland spirit, whose success owes everything to the brothers' characteristically brilliant marketing tactics, emphasizing its virtues as a mixer with orange juice.

GUILD

Guild Wineries & Distilleries, 391 Taylor Boulevard, Suite 110, Pleasant Hill, CA 94523
Tel: (415) 798 7722
Cribari 3 · Guild 3 · Ceremony 5 · Cresta Blanca 10

Guild Wineries, one of the largest in California, offers a wide range, all of them a mixture of pot and continuous still brandies. Some are what they call "rectified", which to the Californians implies the addition of: "a very small amount of smoothening and sweetening material (eg very dark and heavy cream sherry)" where "straight" brandy has only a little caramel added to standardize the colour.

All Guild's brandies are aged in small American oak casks, a combination designed to provide a dry brandy. Guild's own brand is sweet and oaky; Cribari, the same age, is lighter and less oaky (it is matured in used casks); Ceremony is straight and dry; Cresta Blanca is older, heavier, oakier.

KORBEL

F. Korbel & Bros, 13250 River Road, Guerneville, CA 95446-9538 ***Tel: (707) 887 2294***
Korbel

An offshoot of one of the best-known makers of sparkling wines in California, owned by the Heck family who bought it from the Korbels in 1954. The Korbels had been selling brandies since 1889. Today's new brandies – made from a number of grape varieties including Chenin Blanc and Colombard – are bought in from distillers who have to use copper in their continuous stills. The brandies are oak-aged for between three and five years, to provide a rich and smooth brandy.

PAUL MASSON

The Seagram Wine Co, 800 South Alta Street, Gonzales, CA 93926 ***Tel: (408) 675 2481***

Masson is as cagey as the Gallos, only informing us that its brandies are made in pot-stills and matured for between six months and a year. Any other information, apparently, is "proprietary and unavailable for us to give to you".

RMS

Originally a joint venture between Rémy Martin and Jack Davies, who makes Schramsberg, the USA's finest sparkling wine (in late 1986 Rémy bought out its American partner). Like Woodbury, this is a serious attempt to make "double-distilled alembic brandy" in traditional cognac stills. RMS started promisingly, installing eight gleaming stills in a delightful new distillery to the south of the Napa Valley, experimenting with a number of grape varieties. The original blend was overwhelmingly composed of the Colombard, a favourite in Cognac in the 18th century and still used in Armagnac today. They also used Palomino, Chenin Blanc and even a little Muscat. Tasted separately the Muscat was almost tropical in its richness, the Chenin Blanc and the Palomino agreeably flowery. The blend was classic Rémy, rich, dry, albeit shorter than the parent blend.

WOODBURY

Woodbury Winery, 32 Woodland Avenue, San Rafael, CA 94902 ***Tel: (415) 459 4040***

In 1971 Russell Woodbury, already famous for the quality of his fortified wines, set out to make a proper alembic brandy. He uses only the Ugni Blanc grape, double-distils the wine in pot-stills and matures the spirit for 12 years in oak. The result has received the sort of acclaim it deserves, as a serious, if light, competitor to cognac with a lot of the vanilla to be expected from new oak.

LATIN AMERICA

Thanks to the Spanish influence, the Latin Americans have become avid consumers of a wide variety of local brandies. The market is dominated by the Spanish firm of Domecq (q.v.). According to the International Wine and Spirit Record, Domecq's Mexican subsidiary sells a total of 7.5 million cases of brandy: 5.2 million are of Presidente, by far the best-selling brandy in the world. Another 2.2 million are Dom Pedro. But neither these, nor any of the brandies made locally in other Latin American countries by Domecq and its competitors, should form part of this book, since I suspect (details are impossible to come by) they are derived from neutral spirit flavoured with a proportion of grape spirit. The only exceptions are Pisco and the Spanish brandies imported in a concentrated form to be locally diluted and bottled.

PISCO

Pisco is a real brandy, distilled in a pot-still from local grapes. The Peruvians and Chileans both claim they invented the drink during the 17th century. The drink was named after the Pisco tribe who made the earthenware pots in which the brandy was stored. The Peruvian claim is upheld geographically. Pisco is a little port in the southern part of the country from where the drink was originally shipped.

Since the Chileans now produce the best wines in Latin America they can be pardoned for claiming theirs is the best Pisco. As early as 1931 they established strict rules for making Pisco – amongst the first AOC rules in the brandy world. The grapes have to be grown, the wine fermented, and the brandy distilled and stored in Atacama and Coquimbo provinces in the Andean valleys between Santiago, the capital, and the great northern deserts.

Five varieties of grapes are produced, but the best Pisco comes from the Moscatel Rosada and Moscatel de Alejandria (also known as Blanca Italia), both commanding a premium of 15%. The grapes are fermented at 28 to 30°C for five days to produce wine with 12 to 14% alcohol – a process designed to retain as much as possible of the aroma and flavour of the Moscatel grapes.

The stills are modelled on the Charentais pattern, and are small, holding about 15 hectolitres of wine, operating at about 90°C. The wine is distilled only once, to 55 to 60% – although 30% of the liquor is eliminated as heads and tails, blended with fresh wine and redistilled. The newly distilled spirit is diluted with distilled water to between 30 and 43% (depending upon the grade of Pisco) and matured in casks made of oak or rauli (a South American beech) for between two to 15 months.

According to Jan Read, the acknowledged expert on Chilean wines:

> *All Piscos are water-white, except for the Gran Pisco which picks up a little colouring from the wood. The nose and flavour can perhaps best be described as plummy with a hint*

of bitter almonds; Pisco is always dry and the Gran Pisco has a slight overtone of oak because of a longer maturation in small casks. The most popular way of serving Pisco is to shake it up with fresh lemon juice and serve it as Pisco Sour.

And very delicious it sounds too. In 1985 the Chileans expected to produce about 50 million bottles (two thirds of a litre, smaller than most brandy bottles). Pisco is made by 15 firms, who market 24 different brands (often in various grades) including ready-mixed Pisco Sours. The trade is dominated by two firms, Pisco Control and Pisco Capel, who account for 70% of production. They – and two others – have formed a joint company to export Pisco.

Pisco Firms

There are four grades · Seleccion 30% · Especial 35% · Reservado 40% · Gran Pisco 43%

Pisco Control

Cooperativa Agricola Control Pisquera de Elqui.
Pisco Control · Pisco Sotagui · Control sour
A very large cooperative founded in the early 1930s, with 450 members. The headquarters are in La Serena and has six other plants absorbing 36 million kilograms of grapes annually, distilling 3.6 million litres of wine in 30 stills and able to store 3.1 million litres of spirit.

Pisco Capel

Cooperativa Agricola Pisquera de Elqui
Pisco Capel · Capel Sour
Founded by growers in 1964 as a logical consequence to the foundation of an Association of Small Growers in the Elqui Valley, who were fed up with their treatment at the hands of the private distillers. It now has 425 members with premises in the picturesque old town of Vicuna, the capital of the Elqui region. It is about two-thirds the size of Pisco Control, crushing 22 million kilograms of grapes annually, distilling 1.5 million litres of wine in 20 stills and storing 2.5 million litres of Pisco.

AUSTRALIA

The Australians have been prolducing grape spirit for one and a half centuries, originally to reduce a surplus of Sultana grapes. The industry then started to provide grape spirit for the country's fortified wines. Before the end of the 19th century Australia was producing proper brandy, mainly in South Australia, where a local coppersmith had devised an improved type of pot-still.

The country's brandy makers still use the Sultana and the Grenache, but also grapes more suitable for distillation – notably two sherry varieties, the Palomino and the Pedro Ximénez, as well as the Ugni Blanc (called White Hermitage in Australia). Production is strictly regulated: brandy makers may not sell any spirit until it has been matured for two years. Neither may they give the impression that it is "Old" unless it has been matured for at least five years, or "Very Old" unless it has been matured for ten. Moreover, the age on the bottle label has to be that of the youngest brandy in the blend.

Unfortunately, for the brandy makers, a sharp tax increase in the early 1970s permanently reduced production – which is still concentrated in South Australia. It reached a maximum of nearly 4.5m litres per year but is now down to an average of 1.765m litres over the past five years. Fortunately the decline in production has been accompanied by an increase in average quality.

HARDY

Thomas Hardy & Sons, Reynell Road, Reynella, South Australia 5161 ***Tel: (8) 381 2266***
Black Bottle 37·5% 3 · VSOP 37·5% 27
Family-owned winery, established in 1852, which has been making some of Australia's most respected brandies since the 1880s (the spirit is also used for Hardy's ports, by far the best sellers in the country). The grapes for Hardy's brandies come from Riverland in South Australia, and range from Muscat to Riesling. The wines are first distilled in a continuous still and then in one of Hardy's three 12 hectolitre pot-stills. They are then matured in wood. "You must taste them standing on your head to get the full effect" says the company. Such an affected attitude is a pity for they are both serious brandies. The Black Bottle is light both in colour and on the nose. Both aroma and palate are light and fruity, rather dry, like a good cognac from the Fins Bois, albeit with a rather medicinal finish. The VSOP has a lovely vanilly, nutty nose, is full and nutty on the palate, with a hint of nut toffee on the finish.

SAINT AGNES

Angove's Pty, Bookmark Ave (PO Box 12), Renmark, South Australia 5341 ***Tel: (85) 851311***
XXX 3 · Old Liqueur 8–10 · Very Old 18–20
The Angove winery was established a century ago by the newly arrived Dr William Thomas Angove. The family has carried on the tradition ever since. The family's St Agnes brandy is distilled from white Hermitage, Semillon,

Doradillo, Pedro and Sultana. They are double-distilled to less than 83% in one of Angove's three big pot-stills, each holding 82 hectolitres. It is reduced to 50% immediately after distillation, matured in oak, further diluted four months before bottling, when sugar and caramel are also added.

ISRAEL

The Israeli distilleries have the enormous advantage of a tied market, for they are the only producers of kosher brandy. Thus orthodox (and many unorthodox) Jews the world over naturally turn to them.

ASKALON

Askalon Wines – Carmel Zion
Ramle Industrial Zone.
Offices: 8 Gedera St, Tel-Aviv 65245
Tel: (3) 65770677
Askalon 2 · Grand 41 4

Askalon Wines was founded in 1925 by Polish immigrants, the Segal brothers, whose ancestors had distilled in the Russian town of Bobruysk since 1787. Their descendants still run the business. It buys in grapes of many different varieties and distils them in two stills, one continuous, the other a pot-still. The Askalon is a mixture of 55% grape alcohol and 45% lower-strength distillate, while the more luxurious Grand 41, a traditional family product, is 100% lower-strength spirit without any additives. It is rather bland and sweet, with no real grapey feel.

AVDAT

See Carmel.

CARMEL

Société Cooperative Vigneronne des Grandes Caves. Rishon-le-Zion & Zicron-Jacob. Rehov HaCarmel 25, PO Box 2, Rishon-le-Zion 75100
Tel: (3) 942021
Extra Fine 18 months · 777 40% & 42% 3 · Avdat 4–6 · 100 9

A peculiarly Israeli combination. In 1882 Baron de Rothschild first imported French vines and know-how into what was then Palestine. His initiative developed into a major cooperative with 800 members which supplies 85% of the country's grapes. The brandies come from a wide range of varieties and are distilled in six stills: two are continuous, four are pot-stills. All were built in the early days of Israeli independence. The brandies are stored in small (300 litre) oak casks and sweetened with caramel and sugar – although the style has become somewhat lighter recently.

GRAND 41

See Askalon.

SOUTH AFRICA

KWV
XXX · VSOP · 10 · 20 · All 43%

Brandy has a long, albeit rather disreputable, history in South Africa. The early settlers soon planted vines and the first still was established as early as 1672. But for two centuries they produced only a particularly fiery type of marc. This was known variously as dop (short for *dopbrandewyn*, or husk brandy), Cape smoke or *witblits* – the Afrikaans for white lightning.

During the 19th century a handful of wine makers, especially Francis Collison, started to distil proper brandy – a logical consequence of their concern for the quality of the Cape's wines, then much appreciated in Britain. The best brandies were named after their makers, for example, FC for Francis Collison, or "Santy" for Réne Santhagens, a former cavalry officer of French origin who imported the first cognac-type still. By the end of the century the country was drinking 6 million litres of brandy annually (just under a quarter of today's consumption). Most of the brandies were of doubtful quality, to put it mildly: "Immature brandy is the curse of this colony" wrote one historian. Much of the brandy was consumed by the pioneers who fought for control of the gold and diamond fields around Kimberly and Johannesburg, and the mining communities. Although prodigious consumers of liquor, they were generally less concerned with quality (Barney Barnato, one of the richest "Randlords", remained faithful to Cape smoke).

By the mid-1920s proper controls had been imposed upon distillation. A Brandy Board was established and distillation centralized in the newly formed cooperative, Ko-operatieve Wijnbouwers Vereinging van Zuid-Afrika, the wine growers' cooperative, usually known as KWV, which continues to dominate the industry.

No brandy may be sold unless it contains at least 30% of pot-still brandy matured in wood. Some of the remainder can be spirit, but it has to be wine spirit – readily available because KWV has the authority to distil excess wine stocks. An important factor in improving quality is the rebate of duty allowed on brandies which have been distilled in pot-stills and aged for three years – hence known as "rebate brandies". Continuous stills may be used only for wine spirit or for exports. As a result South African liqueur brandies contain up to 95% pot-still spirit and are matured for up to 15 years. The wines come from districts in the Cape where the rich soil gives very high yields – and a wide variety of grapes are used. These include classic varieties like Ugni Blanc and Colombard, but also Cinsaut, Palomino and Sultana.

INDEX

F

G

H

I

J

K

L